Introduction to Patent Litigation

Ralph Terrance Rader

ABA
AMERICAN BAR ASSOCIATION
Intellectual Property
Law Section

Cover design by Jill Tedhams/ABA Design

Printed in the United States of America.

30 29 28 27 26 5 4 3 2 1

ISBN 978-1-63905-773-3

Contents

SECTION II

SECTION III

Introduction

This *Introduction to Patent Litigation* provides an overview of patent litigation. It can be used as an introductory text for training and skill development. It can also be used as a practical reference for corporate managers and business executives who want to be informed on the legal landscape for patent litigation and the terms of art commonly used in patent litigation.

Another purpose for this manual is to assist in developing appropriate management procedures for patent lawsuits. Ultimately, success in a patent lawsuit should not come at any cost. Instead, success should be achieved with reasonable fees and costs that are consistent with corporate goals and budget considerations. It should be an instrument to make money, not spend money. Therefore, this manual is intended to provide a description of the anatomy of a patent lawsuit.

Planning the management of a lawsuit is not easy, because each party has little control over the tactics and strategy of the opposing party or the decisions of the judge. This makes it difficult to estimate a budget or set staffing requirements. Further, even though intellectual property litigation is a well-plowed field, the intellectual property litigation universe is diverse, and repetition of prior litigation strategy or prior lawsuit management may not provide the appropriate or best response to a new lawsuit. Thus, the management of and the strategy for patent litigation continues to be a unique and challenging task.

R. Terrance Rader
raderipconsulting.com

SECTION I

The Decision to File a Lawsuit

Early Risk Management Is Critical for Patent Owner

Management of a lawsuit involves risk management. Risk management for the plaintiff begins before the lawsuit is filed. It includes thoroughly reviewing the client's files and interviewing potential key witnesses. Plaintiff's counsel must develop an outline of the potential vulnerabilities in the case. Questions to be asked include: (a) What is in the prior art? (b) Have searches been conducted? (c) Have statutory bars such as prior uses, sales, and offers of sale been adequately considered? (d) Have any experimental conditions been fully and accurately presented in the patent application? Is the disclosure enabling? Was the best mode disclosed? (e) Has any evidence submitted on patentability, such as evidence under Rule 131 or Rule 132 of the U.S. Patent and Trademark Office Rules of Practice, been accurately presented? (f) Are there any defects in the patent title or exclusive license to the plaintiff? (g) Is this a contributory or inducement to infringe situation? (h) What is the client's exposure to a patent infringement counterclaim? (i) What is the client's exposure to an antitrust counterclaim? (j) What unfair competition issues can be advanced? (k) Are there any specific attorney-client privilege issues? and (l) Has an appropriate control group been formed?

The following items are illustrative of the information that should be elicited during a litigation strategy conference:

(a) Patent validity/enforceability issues: Has any additional adverse prior art been found? Does the patent list all significant prior art? Is the uncited prior art cumulative to the art of record? Does the known prior art invalidate the patent?

(b) Are there any file history problems?

(c) Are there any declaration evidence problems?

(d) Infringement: Does the analysis of the accused product show literal infringement or is infringement under the Doctrine of Equivalents?

(e) Are there any possible counterclaims?

(f) Objectives/goals for the client: (1) Is there a basis for seeking a preliminary injunction? (2) Are lost profits appropriate for damages? (3) Is there evidence of price erosion or inability to raise prices? (4) Is there evidence of lost market share? (5) What is the evidence as to the lack of acceptable noninfringing alternatives? (6) What is an acceptable royalty rate? (7) Can the royalty be based on sales of both the product and "convoyed goods"? (8) Should a complaint be filed but not served to preserve venue selection?

(g) Venue consideration: Do the facts such as ease of discovery, convenience, and jury pools favor a particular venue?

(h) Are there protective order/trade secret/proprietary information issues?

(i) Can technical and economic experts be identified?

(j) Will there be communications to customers regarding the lawsuit, including public announcement considerations?

(k) What is the history (if any) between the parties, including any agreements or settlement proposals?

(l) Which are the parties to be sued?

For Accused Infringer

The preliminary decision to license, litigate, or stop is made in light of a fair assessment of available evidence and legal argument. On questions of validity and enforceability, the evidence available to the accused infringer generally consists of publicly accessible documents regarding the patent, its prosecution history, and prior art. Regarding infringement questions, a comparison should be made between the accused activity and the claim language as interpreted by patent counsel with engineering staff or technical experts. The potential litigant must also consider possible countersuits for patent infringement, antitrust violation, patent misuse, or unfair competition. Based on these preliminary assessments, including the economics involved and business judgment, the potential litigant decides on a course of action.[1]

Settlement is an alternative to litigation. Whether settlement can be reached, however, is primarily within the patent owner's discretion, because the patent owner has no duty to offer a license or any duty to offer a license on less than exorbitant terms. Compulsory licensing does not exist in the United States. The accused infringer attempts to posture itself to negotiate favorable licensing terms. The patent owner's strategy is to bring pressure on the accused infringer in order to secure higher royalties or improvement in the competitive market.

Settlement in patent litigation may avoid possible treble damages under 35 U.S.C. § 284 for "willful infringement." Willful infringement occurs when the infringing acts were committed "without concern for the rights of the patentee" or without a "good faith belief" that the patent is invalid. The patent law imposes an affirmative duty to obtain independent and competent advice of counsel before beginning any commercial activity that might infringe another's patent rights. As increased damages for willful infringement can arise in what appear to be innocent circumstances, the potential litigant must give more than a cursory consideration to settlement in view of the increasing trend in patent litigation to seek and obtain enhanced damages.

In addition to exposure to enhanced damages for willful infringement, the accused infringer may face other liabilities based on the patent owner's lost profits, price erosion, prejudgment interest on damage awards, an award of opposing counsel's attorney's fees, and, most significantly, injunctions.

Good business practice should include conducting a preproduction infringement study before putting a product into commercial production. This infringement study should identify any required redesigning effort before making substantial expenditures for commercial production. In

1. A threatened punitive infringer may bring a lawsuit, i.e., Declaratory Judgment Action. A punitive infringer may also take advantage of one of the Post-Grant Proceedings under the America Invents Action (AIA).

addition, a competent infringement opinion, giving appropriate clearance for a product design, mitigates against a finding of willful infringement and any subsequent litigation involving that product.

However, the opinion should be in writing, and should reflect a competent and thorough analysis, rather than a perfunctory review of the patent and the accused product. It must include careful analysis of the patent's prosecution history and possible claim interpretation issues. Competent advice substantially reduces the risk that willful infringement may be found.

A complete assessment of the risk factors associated with patent infringement cases may not be possible until after the filing of a lawsuit, because much of the evidence may not be known until completion of discovery. Nevertheless, a potential litigant can still assess the strength of witnesses and available evidence before engaging in the lawsuit. For example, witnesses testifying on behalf of an accused infringer need good communication skills to convey the meaning of complex principles and to be able to explain to a non-technically proficient judge or jury the reasons for their business decisions, such that the trier of fact may understand the subject matter.

In patent trials, the burden of proof on various issues follows either the "preponderance of evidence" rule or the "clear and convincing" rule. The party proving a fact by the "preponderance of evidence" rule must prove only that the fact is "more likely than not." The "clear and convincing" rule is a more challenging standard to meet, in between the "preponderance" standard and the familiar standard for criminal trials, "beyond a reasonable doubt." The burden of proof on infringement follows the preponderance rule. On the other hand, the accused infringer has a much higher burden of proof on invalidity or unenforceability questions; i.e., that burden is clear and convincing evidence. With such a high burden to prove invalidity or unenforceability, the accused infringer must have strong evidence; otherwise, the risk of loss may simply be unacceptable.

In addition to risks, legal fees, and expenses, litigation imposes an extraordinary burden on the officers and employees of a party litigant. The greatest burden arises from the amount of time required for consultation with counsel on strategic matters and for responding to discovery demands from the adverse party. An adversary may target deposition officers and directors who can ill afford to take time away from their regular duties and responsibilities to prepare for and participate in depositions. Consultation with the client's officers and employees is also required, not only in preparing for depositions, but also in preparing responses to initial disclosures and discovery requests. Consulting sessions are also needed to learn about the opponent and subject matter of the controversy, and to determine what direction the lawsuit or settlement posture should take. It is typically necessary for a company to dedicate one or more professionals to serve as liaisons between the company and outside counsel to ensure effective and timely communication and preparation.

Document production generally requires employees to search for, compile, identify, and assemble the requested documents. This process may take weeks and can disrupt files and work in progress. Counsel must also screen company documents and mark and/or classify business and technical information, redact wholly irrelevant information, and categorize attorney-client and work product privileged information. It is not uncommon for tens of thousands of documents to be processed for production in an important patent infringement action between head-to-head competitors. An accused infringer's relationship with vendors and/or customers may also be affected by discovery intrusions. For example, vendors or customers may be involuntarily brought into the action by subpoenas for depositions and document production that inevitably cause business disruption and inconvenience. Therefore, the burden of litigation includes, among other things, interference with regular business activities, commitment of substantial time by key personnel for consultation with counsel and preparing for discovery, disruption of files, exposure of confidential information to the other side (unless a protective order is obtained, but then the information is still disclosed to the opposing attorney, the court, and expert witnesses), potential damage to customer and vendor relations, and significant attorney's fees and costs.

Prelitigation Opinions

Patent litigation presents not only the danger of losing, but the additional hazard of multiple damages for the losing "willful" infringer, as well as payment of the opponent's legal fees and expenses. The "exceptional case" and award of attorney's fees apply to the conduct of the losing party, whether that is the plaintiff patent owner or defendant infringer. The losing patent owner may be exposed to liability for the accused infringer's fees and expenses if it is shown that the case was not brought or prosecuted in "good faith." The "bad faith" finding for either the patent owner or the infringer frequently depends on whether the losing party had obtained and relied on a "competent" opinion of counsel, whether or not that opinion was ultimately right or wrong.

The basic requirements for an infringement opinion begin with the question of whether infringement concerns are present. Whether this question is raised by the patent owner or the possible infringer, the same criteria are used to determine what studies are required and what items should be considered for a legal opinion answering the question. The starting point for any infringement opinion is claim interpretation. This implies that whoever renders the opinion must be knowledgeable about U.S. patent law, since the layman's opinion as to what the patent covers carries no weight.

Basic factual materials for claim interpretation include the language of the claims themselves, the written description in the patent specification, and the Patent Office file history or prosecution history of the patent, including prior art references cited in that record. Any competent opinion on infringement must be based on a study of at least these items to determine what the patent claims cover. Only after reaching a proper interpretation of the patent claims can one address the question of whether or not an accused device or composition falls within the scope of those claims.

In determining the meaning of any one claim of the patent, the other claims must also be studied. The existence of dependent claims and different independent claims with varying wording presents implications as to the meaning and scope of the other claims under the principle of claim differentiation. Different claims in a patent are normally interpreted as having a different scope from each other. Further, with regard to the meaning of individual words of a claim, a patentee may be his/her own lexicographer—and the specification becomes the patentee's dictionary. For common words, their ordinary dictionary definition is also relevant, assuming the specification has not accorded a special meaning to such common words as used in the patent claims. Therefore, a thorough reading of the patent specification is essential for claim interpretation.

The next source for the meaning of the claim is the prosecution history of the patent. The law is clear that a patentee cannot solicit allowance of the patent on the basis that the claim language has one meaning and afterward assert that the patent claims mean something else. The clearest case for "prosecution history estoppel" is where the claims were amended during prosecution to overcome a prior art rejection. In this situation, the patentee typically cannot attempt to recapture by claim interpretation that which was given up by the amendment in order to secure allowance of the patent.

After the claims are properly interpreted, the next question is: Does the claim "read on" the accused product? The task here is to determine whether or not each and every limitation of the claim, as properly interpreted, can be found in the accused product or process. The first question is whether each limitation is literally found in the accused item. If so, then the only remaining question is whether or not the claim is valid. If any limitation is not literally found in the accused product, the next question is whether that limitation is infringed under the Doctrine of Equivalents. Under the Doctrine of Equivalents, infringement may be found if an accused device differs from a not-literally-infringed claim limitation in an "insubstantial" way. One way of showing insubstantial difference is if the accused device "performs substantially the same function in substantially the same way to obtain the same result" as the claim limitation in question.

Having analyzed the issue of infringement, the next question is to determine whether the patent claims are valid. Even if it is believed that the claims are infringed, it is normally unwise to enter litigation without considering the defense of patent invalidity. Equally important, the patent owner who is convinced of infringement still needs a competent investigation and opinion on the issue of validity before bringing suit.

Unlike the factual investigation involved in infringement, the issue of patent validity is a multitiered study. The same analysis of the claims, patent specification, and prosecution history of the patent is made with a specific focus on whether there is any reason to challenge the grant of the patent on the record. It must be kept in mind that the same interpretation of the claims must be used when determining infringement and validity. A review of any earlier searches of the prior art should be made for the purpose of determining whether there is any prior art, not made of record with the Patent Office, which might affect the validity of the patent or form a basis for a charge of inequitable conduct and an unenforceability defense. Further, there should be an additional prior art search, which should be as extensive as possible, seeking to find other art not made of record at the U.S. Patent Office that may affect the validity of the claims. Finally, there should be a thorough review of the background and development of the invention with the objective of determining whether there are any other defenses that might be asserted. This investigation is intended to look for potential defects in inventorship, evidence of prior offer for sale or prior public use of the invention, evidence of concealing the "best mode" of practicing the invention, or other public evidence that may be useful in supplementing the information obtained through prior art searches.

Any analysis of litigation risks should extend beyond the infringement and validity determinations. For example, at least the following questions should be asked:

(a) Has the patent been licensed, and if so, is there any problem with the licensing agreements?

(b) What might be a basis for a reasonable royalty if the invention is to be licensed?

(c) What sales volume and what growth in sales has been experienced?

(d) What is the overall market situation and what are the profit margins?

(e) What corporate advertising has been used and what does it say?

(f) Have trade journal articles been published about the invention, and what do they say?

(g) Who are the competitors and what are their sales/marketing/advertising practices for their products?

(h) Has the patent owner made or attempted to make any acquisitions of competitors or followed any course of conduct that may provide the basis for an assertion of an antitrust defense?

From the totality of the analysis, there should be sufficient information to form the basis of a decision to proceed to litigation or not. The magnitude of the investment and expense of the lawsuit (both external and internal) can be estimated and balanced against the magnitude of the potential return or loss.

Commencement of the Lawsuit

A. Who Can Bring a Lawsuit

To bring a lawsuit, an entity must have "standing" to sue. Standing refers to the capacity of a person to act. While the owner or assignee of a patent always has standing to bring a suit, the standing of a licensee depends on a number of factors. For example, exclusive licensees are considered to have standing to maintain a patent suit. On the other hand, a nonexclusive licensee usually does not have standing to bring suit in its name alone. Thus, with respect to nonexclusive licensees, the patent owner usually must also be included as a plaintiff.

B. Where to File Suit

In addition to subject matter jurisdiction, the plaintiff in a patent suit must satisfy the requirement that the court have "personal jurisdiction" over the defendant. This requirement means that the defendant must have "minimum contacts" with the forum. Personal jurisdiction over the defendant can be had in the district where the defendant is incorporated or where the defendant has a manufacturing plant or distribution facility. A more difficult issue of personal jurisdiction arises when infringing goods can be found in the forum without any other real presence of the defendant.

A plaintiff may have a choice of forums in which to bring suit if personal jurisdiction can be established in multiple forums. However, the plaintiff must also satisfy venue requirements. The purpose of venue statutes is to prevent the defendant from having to defend an action in an inconvenient locality. Two separate statutes govern venue: the general venue statute, 28 U.S.C. § 1391, and the patent venue statute, 28 U.S.C. § 1400(b).

With respect to a corporate defendant, the venue requirements are met by suing a corporation in the state of incorporation, at the location of corporate headquarters, or where the defendant is doing business and where there are acts constituting infringement. For individuals, however, venue is proper only in a forum where the person resides or has committed acts of infringement and has a regular and established place of business.

If a patent action is brought in a district where venue is improper, the court may dismiss the action or transfer the action to any district where venue would have been proper. If a defendant does not challenge venue in a timely fashion, venue is waived and the case will proceed as long as the court has personal and subject matter jurisdiction over the parties. Even where venue is technically proper, a party that is inconvenienced by the forum may file a motion with the court under 28 U.S.C. § 1404(a) to transfer the case to another forum where it might have been brought. In considering whether to grant a motion for nonconvenient forum, courts look to the convenience of the majority of the witnesses, the advantages and obstacles to a fair trial in the alternative forum, and other factors favoring an expeditious and relatively inexpensive trial.

C. Who Can Be Sued

All infringing parties are jointly and severally liable for any infringement. Defendants who are jointly and severally liable are each responsible for the full amount of the damages awarded. Thus, the patent owner has the option of suing a single infringer or joining as co-defendants the manufacturer, distributors, and customers. The only limitation is that a patent owner can only recover the full amount of damages once. If a patent owner sues the manufacturer of an infringing device and recovers 100 percent of its damages from the manufacturer, the patent owner cannot then sue the distributors to collect additional damages.

A patent owner may also sue contributory infringers and persons or corporations that induce infringement. Where there are multiple lawsuits pending in different jurisdictions, a patent owner may proceed first against the primary infringer and stay the suit against the secondary infringer until the primary infringement suit has been fully adjudicated. This rule normally applies even where the suit against the primary infringer was filed after the secondary infringement suit. Principles of equity are considered in granting or denying a stay in such instances and the general rule will be ignored where equity demands.

In most instances, a corporation's directors, officers, shareholders, and employees are not personally liable for acts of infringement against the corporation. However, when such a person affiliated with the corporation actively induces or encourages infringement, that individual may be held personally liable.

Except when otherwise required by the rules, a complaint does not need to be verified or accompanied by an affidavit. Nevertheless, Rule 11 of the Federal Rules of Civil Procedure requires that each pleading be signed by at least one attorney unless the party is not represented by an attorney. The attorney's signature is a representation that the attorney has rcad the pleading and that to his/her knowledge, information, and belief, there are good grounds to support it and that the pleading was not presented for delay. In recent years, courts have been more strict in requiring adherence to Rule 11 and lawyers/clients have been sanctioned for filing frivolous and otherwise unmeritorious pleadings.

D. The Complaint

The lawsuit commences when the plaintiff files a complaint with the court. The complaint is typically filed with a summons, and these two documents are then served upon the defendant. Rule 4 permits a delay in service of up to 120 days after the complaint is filed. This time period can be used by the plaintiff to pursue/evaluate settlement options. Upon filing of the complaint, the court clerk will assign a docket number to the case and establish a case file. Under the local rules of the court, the case is typically assigned randomly to a federal judge when the complaint is filed. That judge will preside over the case for the duration of the lawsuit. Many courts also have a magistrate judge practice where a magistrate judge is also assigned to the case and typically rules on routine discovery matters.

The contents of the complaint include (1) a short and plain statement of the grounds upon which the court's jurisdiction depends; (2) a short and plain statement of the claim showing that the pleader is entitled to relief; and (3) a demand for judgment for the relief the pleader seeks. The complaint may be a simple statement of the case. It is sufficient under the Federal Rules if the complaint places the defendant on "notice" of the plaintiff's grievances. Generally, the complaint should allege facts that support every material point in the claim.

The relief sought by the plaintiff should be specifically pled. The plaintiff should plead a request for injunctive relief, compensatory damages, damages for willful infringement, and attorney's fees and costs, if appropriate. Forms of relief available in patent infringement actions include damages pursuant to 35 U.S.C. § 284, which must be at least a reasonable royalty or lost profits. The lost profits can be derived from the profits the patent owner would have made "but for" the infringement, lost profits on actual sales from price erosion due to the infringer's presence in the market, or lost profits from projected sales. In cases of willful infringement, damages may also be increased up to three times the amount assessed by the court or jury. The patent owner should also request prejudgment interest, attorney's fees as provided by Section 285, if applicable, and injunctive relief from the infringement.

Inequitable conduct before the Patent Office is a form of fraud that must be specifically pled. A mere allegation of inequitable conduct will be insufficient. If the plaintiff has insufficient knowledge of facts underlying alleged inequitable conduct at the time the complaint is filed, inequitable conduct should not be included in the complaint. Rather, the plaintiff should amend the pleading once specific information has been developed that permits the standard of particularity for pleading "circumstances constituting fraud" to be satisfied.

If a jury trial is sought, it must be requested in accordance with Rule 38. Either party can demand a jury trial. The rule provides that a separate jury demand may be made "at any time after the commencement of the action and not later than 10 days after the service of the last pleading directed to the issue."

E. The Answer

Rule 12 of the Federal Rules of Civil Procedure provides that within 20 days after service of the summons and complaint, the defendant is required to file an Answer presenting its defenses. The Answer must set forth its position on the allegations in the complaint. All affirmative defenses must be raised in the responsive pleading. Certain defenses, including noninfringement of the patent, absence of liability for infringement, unenforceability, invalidity of the patent, and failure to comply with 35 U.S.C. § 112, must be pled.

In the Answer, the defendant should assert, as a counterclaim, any claim that it has against the plaintiff. The defendant will often include a counterclaim for declaratory judgment of invalidity and noninfringement of the patent asserted by the plaintiff. This step prevents unilateral dismissal of the action by the plaintiff, and therefore provides negotiation leverage to a defendant that has been damaged by a suit based on a patent secured by inequitable conduct or otherwise filed in violation of Rule 11. Counterclaims, like the complaint, set forth the jurisdictional basis for the counterclaim and provide a short statement to give the plaintiff notice of what the defendant's counterclaim is and the grounds upon which it rests.

Cross-claims against a third party are also permitted under Rule 8. The most common cross-claims in a patent action are those seeking indemnification.

There must be a reply to a counterclaim. The reply to the defendant's counterclaim must be served within 20 days after service of the defendant's Answer.

Rule 12 allows a defendant to make a number of defenses by motion. Where appropriate, accused infringers may file a motion to dismiss or a motion to transfer. Courts favor transferring a case to a district where venue is proper over dismissing the case.

Another strategy involves filing an independent action, such as a declaratory judgment action, to provide a basis for urging transfer and consolidation.

Declaratory Judgment Actions

A declaratory judgment action, in accordance with 28 U.S.C. § 2201, permits the potential defendant in a patent dispute to become the plaintiff by taking the initiative in filing suit and asking for a declaration of noninfringement, unenforceability, and/or invalidity. The major requirement in seeking a declaratory judgment is that an actual controversy exist between the parties. For example, the alleged infringement cannot be merely speculative or prospective. Further, the potential infringer must have a reasonable apprehension that the patent owner will bring suit. This typically means that there must have been an actual or implicit charge of infringement so as to put the declaratory complainant under a reasonable apprehension that the patent owner will seek to enforce its patent.

While most declaratory judgment actions are brought by a potential defendant, declaratory judgment actions by patent owners are not unknown, although they are uncommon. A declaratory judgment action can be brought by a patent owner against parties preparing to infringe in the future. If there is a sufficient allegation of substantial preparation and immediacy, a patent owner should be able to seek a declaratory judgment against a future infringer.

Alternative Dispute Resolution Procedures

A. Mediation

In a mediation, an impartial third party, or "neutral," is selected by the parties to assist in settling their dispute. This process is generally entirely private and voluntary; the neutral renders no decision and has no authority to compel any agreement or terms. The neutral may act as a diplomat, meeting with both parties and then separately with each of them to convey countering proposals and generally assist them in reaching mutually agreeable business results in a nonadversarial environment.

B. Mini-Trial Proceeding

A mini-trial is somewhat more formal than a mediation, and involves a presentation by both sides of the merits of their respective cases to a neutral who advises and aids them in negotiating a settlement. A high-level executive from both sides is typically required to be present for the purpose of direct negotiation and also to evaluate the dispute independent of the respective lawyers' opinions. The neutral advisor may be asked to give substantive views of the merits of each side's case and of the likely trial outcome. If no agreement is reached, the parties are then free to proceed to formal litigation, and the entire process will be treated as inadmissible and entirely confidential in any later proceedings.

C. Summary Jury Trial

This is primarily designed for more complex cases and involves a technique for the presentation of counsel's summary arguments and review of prospective trial evidence to a panel of "jurors" who have been selected in much the same manner as for actual trial. After deliberation, the "jury" renders a nonbinding verdict or verdicts, as the parties request, which provides an independent substantive evaluation of the case. Key representatives of the principals are expected to be present for purposes of subsequent settlement negotiations and possibly additional questioning of the jurors regarding the merits of the evidence or the persuasiveness of the attorney's arguments.

D. Neutral Expert Fact-Finder

In patent cases, the issues may turn on specific technical fact questions. In this procedure, the parties agree to an independent neutral expert who, after hearing evidentiary presentations by both sides, renders either binding or nonbinding fact findings. This may lead the parties to a reevaluation of the relative strengths of their cases and lead to a settlement without lengthy litigation and trial.

E. Early Neutral Evaluation

This procedure involves appointment of a neutral, experienced trial attorney or magistrate judge who will hear brief presentations of the merits by both sides and analyze the case from many aspects of expense, discovery, relative merits, etc., in order to facilitate settlement. The neutral usually gives an initial candid evaluation of the probable end result of the case. Assistance may also be given to simplifying discovery.

F. Arbitration

Arbitration ordinarily results from predispute agreements, and can also be entered into at any time by mutual agreement of the parties. One to three arbitrators ("the panel") are typically selected to hear evidence in a more formal proceeding than the foregoing procedures, but still less formal than trial. The panel will render a binding decision (with or without an opinion), which lacks the option of appeal and may be enforced by entry of a judgment. There are various arbitration techniques using established or modified rules for limited discovery and for the receipt of evidence. The process is intended to be shorter, simpler, and less expensive than that of formal court litigation.

G. Private Judges

A magistrate or "rent-a-judge" procedure provides a speedy trial and avoids a crowded court docket, while preserving the formalities of federal procedure and evidence rules, and with application of substantive law. The opinion and decision of the magistrate or private judge may be submitted and adopted as the opinion and judgment of the court itself, and thus with full rights of appeal retained.

SECTION II

The Discovery Process

Pretrial discovery is the phase of a lawsuit in which the parties attempt to gather information about the opponent's facts and contentions on the issues of the case. Discovery can seek anything that appears reasonably calculated to lead to the discovery of admissible evidence. The length of the discovery period (generally six to 12 months or longer) is established by the court in its scheduling order.

The Federal Rules of Civil Procedure provide several tools that can be used to obtain information from opponents and third parties. The following is a general description of these discovery tools.

Discovery Tools

A. Interrogatories

These are written questions sent by one party to another, which must be answered under oath. The party must respond, not only as to those facts known, but also with facts that are reasonably available. Interrogatories are useful for obtaining information including the names of knowledgeable individuals, product identifications, dates of production, and other relevant information. Interrogatories are typically classified into fact interrogatories, contention interrogatories, and expert interrogatories.

Fact interrogatories are useful for obtaining names and addresses of persons who have carried out specified jobs, along with the location of documents. Contention interrogatories are helpful in preparing a case for trial or for settlement discussions. For example, it may be appropriate to ask a patent owner to state the facts that demonstrate a date of invention early enough to overcome an item of prior art or to specify the differences between a patent claim and a prior art reference. Similarly, it is useful to ask a defendant to explain the differences that are contended to distinguish between an accused product and the patent's claims. Expert interrogatories may provide a preview of the opponent's contentions before receipt of the required expert report.

B. Requests for Documents and Things

These are requests from a party to an opposing party to produce any and all documents (not privileged) that may be relevant to (or lead to the discovery of matters relevant to) the issues in the lawsuit for inspection or copying by the requesting party. Inspection of premises and devices may also be permitted.

The request for documents is the most useful discovery tool. Document requests can identify specific documents, but more typically describe categories of documents. The rule for production of documents allows two alternatives for producing documents. Either the documents can be produced "as they are kept in the usual course of business," or they can be organized and labeled to correspond to the categories in the document requests.

Documents may be obtained from third parties by means of a subpoena under Rule 45. The rule authorizes the subpoena to merely require production of the documents, or it may also request the person on whom it is served to appear and give testimony at the same time.

In addition to authorizing inspection of documents, Rule 34 provides for inspection, copying, testing, or sampling of things that are relevant under the standard of Rule 26. This can be important in patent cases that often involve machines, products, and other tangible things. Rule 34 also provides for entry upon land for inspection and other purposes. This means that an opponent's factory, machines, and other facilities can be inspected.

C. Requests to Admit

These are written propositions of fact used for obtaining admission of undisputed facts. The responding party must answer based on knowledge and good faith.

D. Expert Reports

Rule 26 requires a party to provide an expert report for each person "retained or specially employed to provide expert testimony" or for any person "whose duties as an employee of the party regularly involve giving expert testimony." The report is required to include a statement of the opinions to be expressed, the basis and reasons therefore, the data and other information considered by the expert in formulating the opinion, any exhibits to be used, the qualifications of the expert, the compensation to be paid to the expert, and a list of cases in which the expert has testified.

E. Depositions

A deposition is a procedure for taking oral testimony of witnesses, including expert witnesses and nonparty witnesses. Subpoenas may be issued under Rule 45 for nonparty witnesses in any part of the United States. Depositions of a corporation may be taken under Rule 30(b)(6) through persons designated by the corporation to be knowledgeable as to the specified facts or issues. Depositions are frequently used to impeach the testimony of the deponent who later testifies at trial.

F. Protective Orders

Much of the work undertaken by a company involves confidential, trade secret, or otherwise sensitive and proprietary information. Consequently, before producing documents or materials that are in any way confidential or proprietary, the parties must negotiate a suitable protective order. This protective order defines how confidential, trade secret, and proprietary information will be treated and handled by the parties. It will limit those to whom disclosure of such information may occur and may prohibit disclosure of confidential information to employees of the other party. Frequently, the protective order will specifically identify those individuals who can see confidential information. For example, it may be permissible for an in-house attorney who is neither involved with the patent prosecution work of a party nor responsible for managerial or business decision making for that party to be named in the protective order and to have access to the opposing party's confidential information. Protective orders also permit disclosure to trial attorneys for each side, as well as independent experts hired by a party. A protective order may specify at least two categories of documents. The most sensitive may be disclosed only to outside counsel and expert witnesses, while less sensitive documents may be available to selected employees of an opposing party.

G. Claim of Privilege

It is possible to withhold privileged materials from discovery, i.e., attorney-client communications and work product an attorney or party prepared in anticipation of any litigation. The withholding party must still, however, describe the nature of the documents, communications, or things that are being withheld, and provide sufficient information to enable an opponent to assess the applicability of the claimed privilege. It is generally necessary to supply the names of the author and all persons who received the documents or copies, the date, and the subject matter contained in the document, without compromising the confidential information that is withheld.

The Required Disclosures of Rule 26

Rule 26 requires the disclosure of information in documents without waiting for an adversary's formal request. The required disclosures include an identification of individuals who have discoverable information relevant to disputed facts alleged in the pleadings, copies of documents relevant to disputed facts alleged in the pleadings, computation of damages, access to insurance agreements, and the names of expert witnesses who will testify at trial.

Reasons for Taking Depositions

In oral depositions, an attorney asks questions of the witness and both the questions and answers of the witness are recorded by stenographic or other means. The procedure is similar to an examination in a courtroom, except that no judge or jury is present. Oral depositions give the examining attorney a measure of surprise, thereby reducing the likelihood of the witness giving prerehearsed answers. The answers given by the witness may open wholly new areas of inquiry that can be explored before the witness has an opportunity to develop theories or strategies that change from the actual facts of the situation.

Many good reasons exist for taking depositions, including:

(a) Discovering the strengths and weaknesses of the adversary's case, e.g., the facts underlying an infringement claim or invalidity defense, as well as the quality and credibility of witnesses;

(b) Obtaining the opposing party's commitment to positions and commitment to having knowledge or lack of knowledge concerning critical issues;

(c) Discovering facts and obtaining evidence for use at trial including authenticating documents, developing prior art, etc.;

(d) Perpetuating testimony for later use at trial;

(e) Obtaining impeachment and effective cross-examination material for use at trial;

(f) Securing admissions against interest for purposes of supporting a motion for summary judgment, favorable settlement, or victory before the judge or jury; and

(g) Pinning down the adversary's story to avoid being surprised at trial, and to narrow the issues in the litigation.

A discovery deposition should only be taken if the benefit of educating and committing the witness to a story is more important than exposing your case to the other side. Further, a cost-benefit analysis must determine if it makes sense to conduct depositions. Alternative forms of discovery, e.g., requests for production of documents, requests for admissions, interrogatories, and so on, may be more cost effective than oral depositions in preparing for trial. Before embarking on a deposition, it is important to consider your objectives. Admissions or commitments as to knowledge or lack of knowledge obtained from the adverse party by means of depositions can represent the difference between success and failure on summary judgment. It is more difficult for a party seeking to oppose a summary judgment motion to create the necessary issue of fact with respect to its own deposition testimony than it is with respect to affidavits filed on behalf of the party moving for summary judgment. With the limitation on the number of depositions that may be taken by each side, one must be selective in choosing whether to take a particular deposition.

Corporations may be examined in accordance with Rule 30(b)(6) through their officers or managing agents who are acting in those capacities at the time of the examination. The Rule 30(b)(6) deposition notice must describe in detail the matters requested for examination. In response to a Rule 30(b)(6) deposition notice, a corporation must designate one or more officers, directors, managing agents, or other persons to respond to matters for examination identified in the deposition notice.

A Rule 30(b)(6) deposition counts as one deposition even if more than one person is designated to testify. The limitation on depositions and scheduling for discovery is designed to encourage cooperation between the parties during initial discovery.

The best place for a deposition is normally at a location that you control. It may be beneficial to take the deposition at the opposing party's plant or manufacturing facilities, where documents and other physical evidence will readily be available. If the plaintiff is a nonresident, courts have generally held that you can require the plaintiff to attend depositions in the forum where the action has been filed. A subpoena to a nonresident witness must issue from the court for the district in which the deposition is to be taken, generally near the witness's residence. Videotaping of the deposition is effective in sobering a witness or his counsel if disputes are anticipated, and can be useful if the testimony is to be used at trial because the witness is unavailable or is beyond the court's subpoena power.

Thorough preparation and organization are keys to a successful deposition. Because the testimony given in a deposition may determine the ultimate outcome of the litigation, attorneys must carefully prepare and establish goals or objectives to be obtained for each deposition. In general, the preparation should include:

(a) Acquiring in-depth knowiedge of the facts and legal issues involved in the litigation through a review of pleadings, substantive law, and all information provided by the client or acquired during the investigation;

(b) Preparing an outline of points that the attorney intends to cover; however, avoid writing out each of the questions to be asked since this reduces the attorney's ability to be flexible and spontaneous in the interrogation;

(c) Reviewing, organizing, and identifying all documentary or demonstrative evidence intended for use during the course of the interrogation;

(d) Obtaining as much information as possible about the background and temperament of the person being deposed; and

(e) Organizing and digesting references to the current deponent from depositions of others.

Preparing a Witness for Deposition

A deponent should understand what a deposition is and how to conduct himself/herself at the deposition. The attorney should explain that a deposition is a procedure by which an opponent learns about the case by asking questions to be answered under oath, and that it may be used in the litigation for impeachment or for supporting a motion for summary judgment. The preparation of a witness should include:

(a) Understanding who else will be present at the deposition, i.e., opposing counsel, court reporter, and perhaps a representative of the opposing party, but no judge or jury;

(b) Describing the procedure by which the deposition will be conducted, including objections, and explaining to the deponent that he/she should pause before answering a question, which permits time for the defending attorney to object and also encourages the careful consideration of each question by the witness;

(c) Explaining the importance of giving truthful and responsive answers while avoiding argument, speech-making, and volunteering;

(d) Explaining that the shortest answer is normally the best answer, and that the longer the answer, the longer the deposition and the greater the opportunity for opening doors into new cross-examination by opposing counsel;

(e) Discussing as much as possible about opposing counsel's style and personality and reviewing all subject matters on which the deponent is likely to be deposed. The deponent should be interrogated on those subjects to evaluate the deponent's responses before the deposition;

(f) Describing to the witness that he/she should only answer questions that are understood. If there is any doubt, the deponent should ask that the question be clarified or restated. The deponent should only respond to questions that are asked rather than questions the deponent thinks should have been asked. The deponent should also be told to testify only as to those things about which he/she has personal knowledge, not to give speculative answers or opinions and not to volunteer information;

(g) Advising the deponent that he/she may be asked if he/she has met with counsel before the deposition, and to respond truthfully about such meetings. However, discussions between the attorney and client are not discoverable, and the deponent should be advised that he/she will be instructed to not respond to a question which elicits attorney-client communications; and

(h) Explaining to the deponent that during the deposition, the interrogating attorney will usually ask what the deponent has done to prepare for the deposition and whether any documents have been used to refresh the deponent's memory or for the purpose of testifying or in preparation for testifying. It is important to limit or avoid using such documents, if possible, during the preparation process, since the interrogating attorney may request production of those documents.

SECTION III

Substantive Pretrial Motion Practice

Motions should be made in writing that concisely state what relief is requested. A motion is accompanied by a memorandum of law in support of the requested relief. Exhibits in the nature of documents, deposition transcripts, pleadings, declarations or affidavits, or discovery responses may be submitted with the motion. The party opposing the motion submits a memorandum of points and authorities setting forth the reasons why the motion should not be granted. It, too, may include exhibits. Court rules may permit the moving party to file a "reply" to the opposition papers. Moreover, the nonmovant may make a cross-motion on the same legal question, but seeking the opposite relief. Significantly, a motion is never decided by a jury; it is always decided by the court.

Motion for Separate Trial

We frequently see motions to bifurcate or for separate trials in patent litigation. Under F.R.C.P. 42(b), the court may conduct separate trials on any claim, cross-claim, counterclaim, or any separate issue for its own convenience, to avoid prejudice to any party, or to expeditiously and economically resolve the controversy.

A motion to bifurcate may be accompanied by a motion under Rule 26(d) to stay discovery on the issue to be severed. It may be appropriate to separate out single issues for advanced trial and discovery when resolution of the severed issue would dispose of the entire controversy. Examples of dispositive questions in patent infringement actions are whether there were prior sales or public use that would invalidate a patent, as well as issues relating to anticipation, estoppel, laches, inequitable conduct, and the like.

Motions to bifurcate liability and damages issues in patent cases are frequently filed and sometimes granted, often before substantial discovery has occurred. Motions to bifurcate may be accompanied by a motion to stay discovery on the damage phase. If the patent owner fails to establish liability for infringement, then the litigation ends with substantial savings in time and expense without probing into damages issues.

The movant, whether the patent owner or the accused infringer, must show convenience to the court, avoidance of prejudice, and/or judicial economy. Further, a ruling on a motion to bifurcate is discretionary with the court. Instructive on the question of whether a court should bifurcate is the following statement from a federal district court:

> Separation of the issues of liability and damages is appropriate when it promotes coherence at trial and judicial economy. A preliminary finding on the question of liability for the defendant in a case eliminates the need for a damage's inquiry, saving the court and counsel substantial time and the party's significant expense. Moreover, if the liability issue is resolved in the plaintiff's favor, the defendant might well settle the damages to avoid a lengthy trial. [. . .] However, separate trials are not appropriate when the facts are so inextricably interwoven that it is impossible or at least manifestly unfair to the plaintiff to bifurcate.

The first question to be asked is whether the issues sought to be tried are significantly different from one another. On motions to separate damages issues from validity/infringement issues in patent cases, the answer to the question is almost always answered negatively, regardless of whether the patent owner seeks damages based on a "lost profits" or a "reasonable royalty" theory. Normally, both the witnesses and documents differ between the segment of trial relating to validity/infringement issues and the segment of trial relating to damages issues. That is, the validity/infringement issues are technical, whereas the damages issues are obviously financial. However, evidence of commercial success may be relevant to both validity and damages. Likewise, evidence of copying may be relevant to validity, damages, and willful infringement. Thus, there are circumstances in which the validity/infringement issues overlap the damages issues.

Another question is whether the issues are triable by a jury or by the court. Courts do not favor separation in jury trials because of a desire to maintain judicial economy, particularly where the patent owner makes a contention of "willful infringement" that could involve a jury assessment of facts underlying this issue. On the other hand, courts may favor separation of damage from liability issues in complex cases to avoid jury confusion.

Another question is whether prejudice to the party opposing bifurcation may result from bifurcation. If delay in discovery is the primary cause of potential prejudice, a court may permit damage discovery to continue during the liability phase, even though separate trials are granted. There may also be circumstances in which evidence during trial on a potentially separable issue is prejudicial to a party's position on another issue. For example, evidence of willfulness in a patent case may influence the jury's deliberations on liability. Bifurcation of the issue involving the potentially damaging evidence may be appropriate to avoid possible prejudice.

As set forth previously, the grant or denial of a motion to bifurcate and/or stay discovery is discretionary. Therefore, courts may be guided by prior decisions, but should ordinarily treat such motions according to their own preference.

Motion for Preliminary Injunction

One form of relief sometimes available to a patent owner is a preliminary injunction prohibiting the accused infringer from continuing its allegedly infringing activities during pendency of the case. Injunctive relief in patent cases is authorized by 35 U.S.C. § 283, which provides that "[t]he several courts having jurisdiction of cases under this title may grant injunctions in accordance with the principles of equity to prevent the violation of any right secured by patent, on such terms as the court deems reasonable." Such extraordinary relief is afforded because the principal value conferred by the patent statute is the right to exclude others from making, using, or selling the claimed invention (35 U.S.C. § 154). (If monetary relief was the sole relief afforded by the patent statute, then injunctions would be unnecessary and infringers could become compulsory licensees for as long as the litigation lasts.)

A. Basis for Issuance of Preliminary Injunction

The Federal Circuit has held that a four-factor balancing test must be applied to determine whether the grant of a preliminary injunction is appropriate:

(a) Whether the patent owner has a reasonable likelihood of succeeding on the merits;

(b) Whether the patent owner would suffer irreparable harm if the injunction is denied;

(c) Whether the injury to the patent owner, if the preliminary injunction is not issued, outweighs the harm to other parties if the motion is granted; and

(d) Whether the grant of the preliminary injunction is in the public interest.

The Federal Circuit has stated, in weighing these factors, that "equity requires that no one element be dispositive, that each be weighed and measured against the others and against the relief demanded."

1. Likelihood of Success on the Merits

Because of the extraordinary nature of the relief provided by preliminary injunction, the patent owner has the burden of showing a reasonable likelihood of success on the merits with respect to infringement or any invalidity or unenforceability defenses asserted by the accused infringer. This burden differs from the burden of proof at trial, where the burden of proving invalidity and unenforceability by clear and convincing evidence is placed on the party challenging the patent's validity (i.e., the accused infringer).

The Federal Circuit requires a "clear showing" of likelihood of success on the merits. The Federal Circuit has explained that the burden on the movant should be no different in a patent case than for other kinds of intellectual property, where, generally, only a single clear showing is required.

Requests for preliminary injunctions are granted or denied in the early stages of patent litigation. At these preliminary stages, the court does not resolve substantive issues of validity, enforceability, and infringement. Rather, the court makes assessments as to the persuasiveness of the evidence, recognizing that in doing so, it is without the benefit of evidence that may be developed more fully during discovery and elaborated on at trial. Thus, while it is not the movant's burden to prove validity, it must show that the accused infringer's defenses lack substantial merit.

In 35 U.S.C. § 282, "a patent shall be presumed valid" and "the burden of establishing invalidity . . . shall rest on the party asserting . . . invalidity." At trial, the burden of establishing invalidity is placed on the party challenging validity, and the challenging party has the burden of demonstrating, by clear and convincing evidence, that each asserted claim is invalid. It is normal for the accused infringer to challenge validity at the preliminary injunction hearing. Where the evidence presented in support of invalidity raises a substantial issue, the movant seeking a preliminary injunction cannot merely rely on the presumption of validity, which is not evidence that can be "weighed" in determining likelihood of success. The presumption of validity is a procedural device that places the burden of going forward with evidence and ultimate burden of proof at trial on the accused infringer.

A patent owner seeking a preliminary injunction can make a sufficient showing of patent validity in any of three ways: (a) public acquiescence with respect to the patent's validity; (b) a prior adjudication of the patent's validity; or (c) direct technical evidence supporting the patent's validity.

a. Public Acquiescence

Public acquiescence is shown in circumstances in which the patent owner has made, used, or sold its patented product for many years, during which time competitors refrained from making, using, or selling the item. Further evidence of public acquiescence exists where competitors have refrained from making, using, or selling the patented product without first securing a license from the patent owner. Evidence of public acquiescence may be supported or rebutted by other circumstantial evidence. For example, longstanding commercial success of the patented product, the presence of fierce competition in the industry, and a long-felt, but unsolved, need for the product throughout the industry would influence the inference of validity raised by the public acquiescence. Public acquiescence, however, must be based on the public's perception that the patent is valid, and not on other reasons. For example, the district court in one illustrative case refused to recognize public acquiescence after finding that the patent owner's competitors had initially refrained from infringing the patent because of their belief that the market was too small to encourage new entry.

b. Prior Adjudication of Validity

A prior adjudication of a patent's validity against another infringer is generally viewed as demonstrating a strong likelihood of success on the merits. While a district court is not bound by a prior adjudication of validity from a previous litigation involving other alleged infringers, the courts may give considerable weight to such findings, particularly if they were confirmed on appeal by the Federal Circuit. However, the weight to be afforded to a prior adjudication of a patent's validity depends on the similarity of issues of law and fact in the two proceedings. Thus, according to the Federal Circuit, "(a) prior adjudication upholding patent validity after a fully litigated trial, including similar issues of fact and law, contributes strong support to the grant of a preliminary injunction." Further, a prior adjudication need not be a final one to be considered as evidence of likelihood of success on the merits.

c. Proof of Patent Infringement

The patent owner has the burden of proving infringement at trial by a preponderance of the evidence. At the preliminary injunction stage, a patent owner must demonstrate a reasonable likelihood that it will succeed in carrying its burden at trial of proving infringement. However, a patent owner is not required to establish literal infringement to demonstrate a likelihood of success on the merits on the issue of infringement. Instead, the patent owner may rely on the Doctrine of Equivalents as an appropriate ground for supporting a motion for a preliminary injunction. However, reliance on the Doctrine of Equivalents to establish infringement can be viewed by the court as evidence that the patent owner's likelihood of success on the issue of infringement is not clear.

2. Irreparable Harm

To obtain a preliminary injunction in a patent infringement action, the patent owner must show that it will suffer irreparable harm during the course of litigation if the preliminary injunction is denied. "Irreparable harm" is harm that money cannot fix. Clear proof of a patent's validity and infringement has been held by federal district courts sufficient to establish a presumption of irreparable injury because of a patent owner's right to exclusivity:

> This presumption [of irreparable harm] derives in part from the finite term of the patent grant, for patent expiration is not suspended during litigation, and the passage of time can work irremediable harm. The opportunity to practice an invention during the notoriously lengthy course of patent litigation may itself tempt infringers.

Thus, the right to exclude others has been held to constitute a property right that cannot be sufficiently remedied by the award of monetary damages.

If the patent owner cannot make a "clear showing" of both validity and infringement so as to raise a presumption of irreparable harm, it must make a separate showing of irreparable harm. The courts have traditionally accepted an accused infringer's inability to satisfy a money judgment as evidence of irreparable injury. Further, loss of market share during protracted litigation may constitute the type of harm that would justify the extraordinary relief afforded by preliminary injunction. Moreover, courts have found that irreparable harm occurs where, in the absence of an injunction, other potential infringers will be encouraged to infringe.

In a case involving the issue of harm, a federal district court found that there already was substantial competition and that the accused infringer had substantial market presence. Further, the technology in issue changed quickly and there was much research being done. The district court stated:

> It is entirely possible that by the time the litigation is finished, the value of the patent may be gone. Its value, insofar as it could help [the movant] establish a market position, create business relationships, and

> thereby gain a foothold in the market, may be lost. The patent might still be there, but the technology might well have bypassed it, or have found alternatives that are not currently available. In that case, [the movant's] opportunity to establish itself in the market will have been destroyed.

The presumption of irreparable harm is rebuttable. Even upon a clear showing of a patent's validity and infringement, a court should still examine several additional factors before determining whether irreparable harm exists. Evidence that may be presented by the opposing party includes (a) a delay by the patent owner in seeking a preliminary injunction; (b) the granting of licenses by the patent owner; and (c) cessation of infringing activity by the accused infringer.

a. Delay in Seeking an Injunction

A patent owner's delay in filing a motion for preliminary injunction may provide a defense for an accused infringer. By establishing a laches or equitable estoppel defense, an accused infringer may rebut an assumption of irreparable harm. A defendant has the burden of proving (a) the plaintiff delayed filing suit for an unreasonable and inexcusable length of time from the time the plaintiff knew or reasonably should have known of its claim against the defendant; and (b) the delay operated to the prejudice or injury of the defendant. A patent owner's delay in seeking a preliminary injunction does not operate to rebut a presumption of irreparable harm as a matter of law. The Federal Circuit has explained that the period of delay is simply one factor to be considered in deciding whether irreparable harm exists:

> Although a showing of delay may be so significant, in the district court's discretion, as to preclude a determination of irreparable harm, a showing of delay does not preclude, as a matter of law, a determination of irreparable harm. A period of delay is but one circumstance that the district court must consider in the context of the totality of circumstances.

The patent owner may avoid a laches defense by establishing good cause for its delay. The Federal Circuit has held that a patent owner's delay in seeking a preliminary injunction was excused given its particular situation and financial resources. Laches may also be avoided if a patent owner's delay was the result of an attempt to resolve its dispute with the accused infringer through means other than litigation.

b. Granting of Licenses

Extensive licensing by the patent owner has been construed by some courts as a factor weighing against a finding of irreparable injury. The granting of licenses has been interpreted as being incompatible with the emphasis on the right to exclude that forms the basis for injunctive relief.

c. Cessation of Infringing Activity

Cessation of infringing activity by an accused infringer may also rebut a presumption of irreparable injury. For example, the Federal Circuit has held that premotion cessation by defendant of its production of accused product established the absence of irreparable harm.

3. Balancing Harm to Movant Against Harm to Nonmovant

The courts are typically wary that "a preliminary injunction improvidently granted may impart undeserved value to an unworthy patent." Notwithstanding the hardship that a preliminary injunction might cause an alleged infringer, the Federal Circuit does not require that the balance of hardships tip in the patent owner's favor. The balance of hardships is only one factor to be considered.

Some courts have found that the balance of hardships tips in the accused infringer's favor where the accused infringer's activities would have a relatively small impact on the patent owner. For example, the accused infringer merely used an infringing device without actually competing with the patent owner, or the accused infringer was a small company. Other circumstances tipping the balance of hardships in the accused infringer's favor include (a) the patent owner holds a large percentage of the market; (b) the accused infringer's small presence in the field; (c) the accused infringer's personnel would have to be laid off if an injunction were granted; and (d) the serious and adverse effect on the accused infringer's ability to establish a market if its product was later found to be noninfringing. However, courts are less likely to show compassion for an accused infringer who ignores the risk of being enjoined. For example, in one case, the accused infringer continued to market its accused device without taking any financial steps to protect itself, despite specific knowledge that the patent owner had accused the device of infringing and planned to continue its infringement suit, which had been pending for several years. The court there found that any hardship to the accused infringer was largely self-inflicted.

4. Effects on the Public Interest

Whether the grant of a preliminary injunction is in the public interest focuses on whether there is some critical public interest that would be injured by granting preliminary relief. One example of a critical public interest that weighs against granting preliminary relief is the public's interest in the availability of an accused device that has an impact on the public welfare. The Federal Circuit held that the district court did not abuse its discretion in excluding an accused infringer's cancer and hepatitis test kits from a preliminary injunction based on the public interest in maintaining the availability of these kits. Another public interest that may weigh against the grant of a preliminary injunction is the public interest in promoting competition. Notwithstanding the public's interest in the protection of rights secured by valid patents, the court's public interest analysis generally focuses on whether some critical public interest exists that would be harmed by granting preliminary relief.

B. Evidentiary Hearing

F.R.C.P. 65(a) expressly requires that notice be provided to an adverse party before the issuance of a preliminary injunction. The right to an evidentiary hearing regarding entry of a preliminary injunction is implicit in the notice requirement of Rule 65(a). The Federal Circuit has stated that, as a rule, a preliminary injunction should not issue on the basis of affidavits alone. The Federal Circuit has cautioned that the danger of disturbing the balance between antitrust concerns and the need to protect intellectual property rights may be great where the plaintiff occupies a dominant position in the relevant market. However, where the magnitude of the inquiry would make a hearing impractical, a preliminary injunction may issue on the basis of affidavits alone.

The scope of an evidentiary hearing for a preliminary injunction may vary. Formal evidentiary hearings tend to resemble actual trials, with each side presenting evidence through live direct and cross-examination. The benefit of presenting evidence through witnesses is especially important in the trademark and patent area, where a plaintiff can totally prevent the conduct of a defendant's business through the use of these injunctions.

The availability of preliminary injunctions provides patent owners with a powerful procedural tool for enforcing their rights. A firm grasp of the four-factor balancing test is critical because the required evidentiary showing to obtain preliminary injunctive relief is demanding.

Motions for Summary Judgment

A motion for summary judgment is an attempt to resolve the entire case or portions of it prior to trial. The burden is on the moving party to demonstrate that no material facts in the case are in dispute and that judgment is proper as a matter of law. Although a motion for summary judgment is typically filed near or after the close of discovery, the movant may move for summary judgment much earlier. Motions for summary judgment may be supported by affidavits, depositions, answers to interrogatories, or other admissible evidence. The opposing party must respond with countervailing evidence to avoid the entry of judgment. It is not sufficient for the opposing party to respond simply by disagreeing with the moving party's proffered evidence. Motions for summary judgment are frequently considered as a device for narrowing factual contentions.

The Supreme Court encouraged the use of summary judgment by the courts in deciding a trilogy of cases in 1986. The Court restated the importance of summary judgment even in complex cases and placed the burden upon the party opposing summary judgment to come forward with evidence that a genuine issue of material fact exists. Prior to the Supreme Court's trilogy of summary judgment cases, the Federal Circuit had already approved the use of summary judgment in patent cases.

A. Summary Judgment for the Patent Owner

While summary judgment should be equally available to the patent owner and accused infringer, the patent owner rarely obtains a summary judgment of validity. By raising issues of fact concerning the nature and content of the prior art, differences between the prior art and the patent claims, and the level of ordinary skill in the relevant art, an accused infringer normally can defeat the patent owner's summary judgment motion for validity. The patent owner can, however, seek a summary judgment of infringement. By disposing of the infringement issue prior to trial, the issues at trial are narrowed, thereby simplifying the trial.

B. Summary Judgment for the Accused Infringer

Whether the accused infringer is a defendant in a patent infringement case or the plaintiff in a declaratory judgment action, the accused infringer is more likely to prevail on summary judgment than the patent owner. Summary judgments of invalidity are more difficult to obtain than summary judgments of noninfringement. Where summary judgments of invalidity are granted, the accused infringer has a greater chance of prevailing in an invalidity summary judgment motion based on one of the statutory bars under 35 U.S.C. § 102 than one based on "obviousness" under 35 U.S.C. § 103. Summary judgments based on a showing of unenforceability because of inequitable conduct are quite rare. Those cases involve contested factual issues concerning intent. Summary judgments of noninfringement are the most commonly granted motions in patent cases. In almost all cases of summary judgment for noninfringement, there has been a clear omission of one or more elements from the patent claims, a substantially different mode of operation, or a clear prosecution history estoppel.

1. Summary Judgment of Invalidity

The Federal Circuit has affirmed several district court judgments granting summary judgment of invalidity under the provisions of 35 U.S.C. §§ 102 and 103. For example, the Federal Circuit affirmed a summary judgment of invalidity under 35 U.S.C. § 103, as follows:

> While the ultimate issue of patent validity is one of law, the conclusion that an invention would not have been obvious is dependent upon several basic factual inquiries. Therefore, a district court can properly grant as a matter of law, a motion for summary judgment on patent invalidity when the factual inquiries into obviousness present no genuine issue of material facts.

The Court affirmed the district court's decision of summary judgment even though the district court had resolved that the secondary considerations (long-felt need, failure of others, commercial success) weighed in favor of the patent owner. The Court agreed that the secondary considerations did not carry sufficient weight to override a determination of obviousness based on the closeness of the prior art.

On the other hand, the Federal Circuit has also reversed a number of summary judgment adjudications of invalidity. For example, the court reversed a decision that the best mode of the invention had been withheld. The court determined that the omitted information was no more than a routine manufacturing choice. In another case, the Federal Circuit reversed a decision that an earlier design patent did not provide a sufficient written description under 35 U.S.C. § 112 for the later continuing utility patent to obtain an earlier effective filing date. Another example is found in a case where the Federal Circuit reversed a summary judgment of invalidity based on 35 U.S.C. § 103. The Court stated that the district court had improperly relied on a reexamination proceeding and erroneously determined that Rule 131 affidavits had been insufficient to antedate prior art:

> In an infringement suit before a district court, the invalidity of a patent under 35 U.S.C. § 103 must be decided on the basis of prior art adduced in the proceeding before the court. The issue cannot be decided merely by accepting or rejecting the adequacy of the positions taken by the patentee in order to obtain a certificate of re-examination for the patent.
>
> A continuing Graham analysis of the pertinent prior art must precede a holding concerning the obviousness of the patented invention. In addition, the fact that the Examiner initially rejected Greenwood's claims under 35 U.S.C. § 103 is not proof of obviousness in the infringement action before the District Court . . . since the proper

Graham analysis was not made by the district court, the summary judgment of obviousness under 35 U.S. C. § 103 must be vacated.

In summary, the Federal Circuit's decisions demonstrate that if there is no genuine dispute of the material facts, a summary judgment of invalidity can be obtained, although the presumption of validity must be overcome by clear and convincing evidence.

2. Summary Judgment of Infringement

As set forth previously, the Federal Circuit has affirmed summary judgments of infringement. For example, the Federal Circuit has confirmed the district court's decision that assignor estoppel precluded the defendant from challenging the validity of the patent. Decisions from the Federal Circuit demonstrate the importance of presenting admissible evidence to rebut the prima facie case established by a party moving for summary judgment.

3. Summary Judgment of Noninfringement

The Federal Circuit has affirmed summary judgment adjudications of noninfringement even when the trial court does not explicitly set forth findings and conclusions to support its decision on summary judgment. The Federal Circuit has affirmed summary judgment adjudications of noninfringement concerning both literal infringement and infringement under the Doctrine of Equivalents, both before and after the *Markman* decision,[1] where the nonmovant's evidence does not present a question of material fact that requires submission to a jury.

4. Summary Judgment of Laches and Equitable Estoppel

In reversing a district court's grant of summary judgment on both laches and equitable estoppel, the Federal Circuit has clarified the principles of laches and equitable estoppel applicable in a patent infringement suit. Initially, the court noted that the defenses of laches and equitable estoppel are matters committed to the sound discretion of the trial judge and

---

1. Markman v. Westview Instruments, Inc., 52 F.3d 967, 979 (1995).

that the trial judge's decision should be reviewed under the abuse of discretion standard. But the Federal Circuit concluded that the lower court had improperly shifted the ultimate burden of persuasion to the patent owner to negate the prima facie defense of laches, and therefore, the district court's grant of summary judgment on the laches defense was in error.

With respect to equitable estoppel, the Federal Circuit also determined that the district court erred in granting summary judgment.

> Moreover, silence alone will not create an estoppel unless there was a clear duty to speak, or somehow the patentee's continued silence reinforces the defendant's inference from the plaintiff's known acquiescence that the defendant will be unmolested. Finally, on summary judgment, such inference must be the only possible inference from the evidence.

Thus, while the defenses of laches and equitable estoppel are still viable defenses in patent cases in which the facts show an unreasonable delay in excess of six years, the Federal Circuit clarified the principles of laches and equitable estoppel and the burdens of proof.

5. Summary Judgment of Inequitable Conduct

The Federal Circuit has affirmed a summary judgment of unenforceability for inequitable conduct where deceptive affidavits were filed under Rule 132, to obtain allowance of the patent-in-suit, and sales information prior to the critical date was withheld.

Significantly, this case laid to rest the contention that a party is entitled to a jury trial on the issue of inequitable conduct.

> Finally, before addressing the merits of the district court's ruling on inequitable conduct, we must correct repeated statements by Paragon that it was deprived of a jury trial on this issue. A number of Supreme Court cases do refer to intent as an issue to be resolved by a jury. However, on closer analysis, it is clear that the Supreme Court's statements have no applicability in the context of the inequitable defense. The defense of inequitable conduct in a patent suit, being entirely equitable in nature, is not an issue for a jury to decide. A patentee has no right to a jury trial respecting the factual element of culpable intent as part of the defense of inequitable conduct.

With respect to the inequitable conduct resulting from the failure to inform the Patent Office of prior sales, the Federal Circuit stated:

> As further ground for inequitable conduct, the district court included the patentee's failure to disclose to the examiner the pre-critical date commercial sales of the patented device. Paragon asserts that the record shows at least a factual issue respecting the element of intent to deceive the examiner by not disclosing these sales.
>
> A party charging inequitable conduct may make a prima facie case by showing an unexplained violation of the duty of candor. In a response or denial, the patentee may set forth facts which show that under the circumstances as the applicant and/or his attorney perceive them, an inference of wrongful intent should not be drawn. Facts showing, for example, their good faith mistake in the law or the facts or mere negligence may be enough to raise a genuine dispute.
>
> Absent explanation, the evidence of a knowing failure to disclose sales that bear all the earmarks of commercialization reasonably supports an inference that the inventor's attorney intended to mislead the P.T.O. The concealment of sales information can be particularly egregious because, unlike the applicant's failure to disclose, for example, a material patent reference, the examiner has no way of securing the information on his own.

Thus, the Federal Circuit is willing to extend summary judgment into areas normally thought to be forbidden. However, many courts still find summary judgment to be inappropriate to resolve the issue of intent with respect to the defense of inequitable conduct.

Properly used, summary judgment can be a powerful tool for the patent owner or the accused infringer in a patent infringement suit. It can dispose of or simplify complex and costly litigation well before trial. The Supreme Court's trilogy of summary judgment cases served to confirm the Federal Circuit's prior decisions and to provide broad encouragement for using summary judgment as a vehicle to assist the courts in sorting through the widely diverse issues that typically arise in a patent infringement suit.

SECTION IV

Patent Trial Preparation

The trial of a patent case will inevitably include consideration of at least two issues: (a) Is the patent valid? and (b) Has the alleged infringer actually infringed the patent in-suit? Patent validity may involve consideration of whether the patented invention is anticipated under 35 U.S.C. § 102, and whether it was obvious, in view of the prior art, under 35 U.S.C. § 103. Prior art, of course, includes patents, published literature, and other available information that was in existence at the time the invention was made.

As set forth in *Panduit Corp. v. Dennison Manufacturing Co.*,[1] the first determination in assessing patent validity under 35 U.S.C. § 103 is the pertinent prior art and what has been claimed:

> Analysis begins with a key legal question: What is the invention claimed? Courts are required to view the claimed invention as a whole, 35 U.S.C. § 103 . . . another key preliminary legal inquiry is: What is the prior art?[2]

The trier of fact must also go through the factual inquiries set forth in *Graham v. John Deere Co.*,[3] which includes determining the scope and content of the prior art, differences between prior art and the claimed invention, resolving the level of ordinary skill in the prior art, and reviewing objective evidence, normally referred to as "secondary considerations." The last inquiry may include such elements as:

> commercial success due to the invention, a failure of others to arrive at the invention, long-felt need, movement of those skilled in the art

1. 810 F.2d 1566 (Fed. Cir. 1987).
2. *Id.* at 1597.
3. 383 U.S. 1, 17–18 (1966).

in a different direction, skepticism of experts, copying of the invention in preference to the prior art and other events proved to have actually happened in the real world.[4]

With regard to infringement issues, it is also necessary for the court and each member of a jury, where a jury is involved, to understand the patented technology, as well as the nature of the allegedly infringing apparatus or process, including how it operates, how it is constructed, and how the patent claims "read on" the allegedly infringing device or method. A patent owner may also be required to proceed under the Doctrine of Equivalents to prove a case of infringement. If this is necessary, the trier of fact is led through what is disclosed in the patent and then educated as to what constitutes equivalents of the claimed invention. The alleged infringer has the opposite task of proving why there is no infringement or why the patent is invalid or unenforceable.

Since the judge or jury is faced with prior art patents, technical literature, and other forms of technical and scientific information, each party has the task of educating to produce both understanding and comprehension. This is the primary reason why expert witnesses are important in patent cases.

Testimony by Experts

Under Federal Rule of Evidence 702, an expert can be permitted to testify about anything that "will assist the trier of fact to understand the evidence or to determine a fact in issue." The primary consideration for testimony under Rule 702 is "helpfulness." Rule 702 addresses the qualifications that can enable persons to testify as "experts." People who do not have formal education but have had practical experience within a field may testify as experts, in addition to those who have formal education.

Rule 703 of the Federal Rules of Evidence sets forth the nature of the evidence, information or material, upon which an expert can base his/her opinion. There are three sources of facts or data upon which the expert can rely: (a) facts or data perceived directly and independently by

4. *Panduit* at 1598.

the experts; (b) facts or data made known to the expert at trial; and (c) facts or data made known to the expert before the trial.

Rule 704 of the Federal Rules of Evidence allows an expert to provide an opinion on the ultimate issue of fact. Under Rule 704, opinion testimony, otherwise admissible, is not objectionable because it embraces an ultimate issue to be decided by the trier of fact. In patent cases, the issues of validity, invalidity, obviousness, nonobviousness, infringement, noninfringement, willfulness, and other issues are all matters that can be considered as "ultimate issues" to be decided by the trier of fact.

Rule 705 of the Federal Rules of Evidence permits an expert to testify about an opinion, together with giving reasons therefore, without prior disclosure of the underlying facts or data. The expert may set forth qualifications and then proceed directly to the opinion, followed by an explanation of the basis for that opinion.

Rule 706 (Court Appointed Experts) of the Federal Rules of Evidence recognizes that there are instances where the court needs its own assistance in dealing with technical issues. A busy trial court faced with complex technology may require independent education or analysis if it is to understand the technology before the trial. For example, a court may find it helpful in determining a motion for summary judgment in a patent case to obtain an independent explanation of the technology and assistance in understanding the positions of the parties.

Types of Experts in a Patent Case

A. Technical Experts

A technical expert in a patent case can include the inventor or an independent expert who has worked in the field or has some other basis for having the necessary familiarity with the technical subject matter. Technical experts may perform one or more of the following functions: (a) perform tests or undertake inspections concerning the accused product or process; (b) educate the court and jury as to the underlying technology; and (c) testify on a broad range of patent issues.

Technical experts may be utilized to conduct tests or inspections of the accused or patented product or process or even of a prior art product or process. These tests and inspections can be particularly desirable when the patent covers a process or method. The patent claims may specify steps or parameters that are not readily ascertainable without a physical inspection or test. The insight the expert gains from the inspection or test may be the basis for testimony at trial.

Patent infringement is an issue of fact. The Federal Circuit has permitted expert testimony on infringement, as long as it explains, in sufficient detail, whether the accused product or process meets every claim limitation literally or under the Doctrine of Equivalents. Expert testimony on the Doctrine of Equivalents may convey how the patent owner compares the "function-way-result" of the elements of the claimed invention with those elements of the accused product or process, or otherwise explain whether the differences are substantial or insubstantial.

At trial, it is normal to have technical experts, including the inventor, explain the invention, underlying technology, and prior art. The patent owner frequently explains how the invention is an important advance over selected prior art and how the accused product or process meets the limitations of the claims in issue, either literally or under the Doctrine of Equivalents. The patent owner's presentation often includes one expert applying the infringed claims to the accused product or process, with demonstrative evidence for illustrating the expert's testimony.

If infringement under the Doctrine of Equivalents is asserted, the technical expert may testify about "insubstantial differences," "function-way-result," and "known interchangeability" between limitations in the claims and corresponding elements in the accused product or process. If prosecution history estoppel is asserted, the technical expert may also testify as to the meaning of technical terms used in the prosecution history and the claims.

Expert testimony concerning the underlying factual inquiries of obviousness is permissible. Technical experts have been allowed to testify concerning (a) the general knowledge of a person of ordinary skill in the pertinent art; (b) a review and explanation of prior art and a comparison of the differences or similarities between the prior art and the claims; (c) the teachings of prior art references and the presence or absence of suggestions in the prior art for combining the prior art; (d) whether a given prior reference is enabling, and whether one skilled in the art would understand it to be so; (e) whether modifications of prior art were known to persons skilled in the art; and (f) whether one skilled in the art would be motivated to combine the pertinent prior art references.

Expert testimony related to the so-called secondary considerations of obviousness, including long-felt need, failure of others, and commercial success, has been allowed. With respect to means-plus-function claims, expert testimony has been permitted with respect to the structure referred to in a means-plus-function limitation, the prior art containing that structure, and whether the function of that structure is the same or equivalent to the function of the structure in the prior art.

The Federal Circuit has approved the use of expert testimony on the issue of inequitable conduct, including testimony on the issues of intent to deceive and materiality of information that was not disclosed and opine on what that information teaches one of ordinary skill in the art.

Since the *Markman* decision,[5] the courts have permitted expert evidence on the meaning of the claim terms to be considered in coming to a conclusion as to a meaning of the claims. A need for expert testimony may arise in connection with the *Markman* hearing. The Federal Circuit has ruled that the primary sources for construing patent claims are the claims themselves, the specification and the prosecution history, i.e., the so-called intrinsic evidence. Where ambiguity remains after consideration of the intrinsic evidence, "extrinsic evidence," such as dictionaries, treatises, and prior art, may also be considered. Expert testimony may also be helpful to the Court in arriving at an understanding of the technology and how the intrinsic evidence would be understood by a person of ordinary skill in the art.

5. In 1995, the Federal Circuit found that construing the meaning of language in a patent claim is solely a question of law to be determined by a judge, not a question of fact for a jury. In finding that the meaning of language in a patent claim is solely a question of law, the Federal Circuit found in *Markman v. Westview Instruments, Inc.*, 52 F.3d 967, 979 (1995), that "competitors should be able to rest assured, if infringement litigation occurs, that a judge, trained in the law, will similarly analyze the text of the patent and its associated public record and apply the established rules of construction, and in that way arrive at the true and consistent scope of the patent owner's rights to be given legal effect." The *Markman* decision requires that the court interpret the language in a patent claim and then instruct the jury on its meaning. It has become common practice for the court to make a *Markman* determination before ruling on any motions for summary judgment regarding infringement or validity.

Expert testimony or affidavits and expert reports have been used in connection with preliminary injunction and summary judgment motions in patent lawsuits. In many instances, technical experts have been utilized to explain the technology, interpret prior art and claim language, and otherwise speak to substantive issues like infringement or obviousness. However, the decision in *Markman* has created uncertainty and inconsistency with respect to the proper role of experts, including technical experts, in connection with the patent claim construction portion of patent cases.

B. Legal Experts

A patent law expert is an individual with specialized knowledge, training, education, and experience in Patent Office practice and patent law. Such an expert may also have a technical background that encompasses the technology involved in the lawsuit. The role of patent experts in claim interpretation has become disfavored, especially in view of the *Markman* decision. However, patent experts still have a role in explaining Patent Office procedure and patent practice and analyzing the prosecution history of the patent-in-suit.

At trial, it is normal for the testimony of a technical expert to be followed by a patent law expert. The patent law expert explains patent practice and procedures and specific relevant aspects of the patent file history and prior art considered during the prosecution. The patent expert may also provide testimony relevant to the legal issue of prosecution history estoppel. Courts differ substantially on the extent to which they will permit a patent law expert to opine on prosecution history estoppel and the ultimate issue of infringement.

Since "obviousness" under 35 U.S.C. § 103 is ultimately a question of law, an expert's opinion (whether it be a legal or technical expert) on the ultimate conclusion of obviousness is neither required, controlling, nor even evidence. In practice, a technical expert normally addresses the underlying factual considerations and may render an opinion that the invention would have been obvious (or not obvious) to one of ordinary skill in the art at the time the invention was made. The technical expert's testimony may then be supported with testimony of a patent law expert who discusses relevant points from the prosecution history that relate to obviousness, while relying on the testimony of the technical expert and perhaps other witnesses, including the inventor. Thus, the patent law expert's testimony should focus more on technical issues as applied to the prosecution history of the patent-in-suit.

Where an exculpatory opinion authored by an attorney for the accused infringer is offered to negate a charge of willful infringement, a patent law expert may be permitted to critique the opinion as to its thoroughness and compliance with generally practiced standards for that type of legal work.

In summary, a patent law expert is desirable to explain to the judge or jury what transpired in the Patent Office and whether the prosecution of a particular patent was regular or irregular. Patent experts have been widely used and their testimony is generally accepted, even though the testimony may include an explanation or application of law. On the other hand, legal experts who merely give testimony that amounts to a lecture on patent law or a legal argument may be excluded from testifying at trial.

C. Damages Experts

Damages in patent cases are determined if the liability phase has been concluded in favor of the patent owner and the patent has been held valid, enforceable, and one or more of its claims has been found to be infringed by the alleged infringer. Economic experts can testify during trial (if the case is not bifurcated) on the profits lost by the patent owner, assuming the measure of damages is "lost profits," and on the value of the patent when the measure of damages is a "reasonable royalty." A damages expert can be helpful in explaining how licenses are negotiated, if the measure of damages is a reasonable royalty. The testimony of the expert can explain how a patent owner has been damaged, establish the basis for marginal costs and incremental profits, and explain and demonstrate how the economic facts support the level of damages being sought by the patent owner. Conversely, the alleged infringer will present its own economic expert whose role is to challenge the basis of the patent owner's economic expert's calculations.

The damages phase of a patent lawsuit may involve testimony on the amount and methodology of computing damages, and, if lost profits are sought, the appropriateness of awarding damages. There are different categories of damages experts, including (a) accounting experts; (b) patent licensing experts; (c) industry experts; and (d) economists. Further, technical experts may provide testimony on issues that relate to elements of damages, such as the availability and suitability of noninfringing substitutes.

Accounting experts normally compute the amount of damages based on appropriate accounting practices. Licensing experts present evidence with respect to the reasonable royalty measure of damages by applying the factors of *Georgia-Pacific Corp. v. United States Plywood Corp.*[6] Industry experts normally testify on issues relating to the patent owner's entitlement to lost profits. Finally, economists normally deal with issues addressed by industry experts, such as analyzing the "relevant market" and dealing with lost profits theories based on price erosion or market share.

There are two measures of permissible damages in patent litigation: lost profits and reasonable royalty. In order to recover lost profits, the patent owner must show that the infringer actually caused the economic harm for which the owner seeks compensation. Lost profit damages include lost profits due to diverted sales, price erosion, and increased expenditures caused by the infringement.

The typical way for a patent owner to prove entitlement to lost profits damages is the test set forth *in Panduit Corp. v. Stahlin Bros. Fiber Works, Inc.*[7] The *Panduit* test requires that a patent owner establish (a) demand for the patented product; (b) absence of acceptable noninfringing substitutes; (c) the patent owner's manufacturing and marketing capability to exploit the demands; and (d) the amount of profit it would have made.

The patent owner is entitled to no less than a reasonable royalty. This measure of damages is "based upon a hypothetical negotiation between the patentee and the infringer when the infringement began." The trier of fact considers what royalty would have been agreed upon

6. 318 F. Supp. 1116, 1121 (S.D.N.Y. 1970).
7. 575 F.2d 1152, 1156 (6th Cir. 1978).

as a consequence of arms-length negotiations between those parties. In *Georgia-Pacific*, the court set forth a list of 15 factors to be considered in determining a reasonable royalty. The patent statute, i.e., 35 U.S.C. § 284, itself contemplates a role for experts in assessing damages by providing: "[t]he court may receive expert testimony as an aid to the determination of damages or of what royalty would be reasonable under the circumstances."

Normally, the parties rely on industry or patent licensing experts in determining the reasonable royalty measure of damages. The licensing expert typically applies the *Georgia-Pacific* factors and his/her knowledge and experience in drafting and negotiating license agreements in the pertinent field. In making the royalty determination, it is appropriate to look to other licenses of the parties and other licensing practices in the pertinent industry, as well as the testimony of witnesses on commercial success or the pioneering nature of the patented invention.

Damages experts may also be employed in assessing lost profits, depending on the facts and circumstances of the case. If there is a two-supplier market, or if the damages are strictly tied to lost bids for specialized contracts, the parties may employ an accounting expert as well as industry and technical experts. If "lost profits" is the appropriate measure of damages, a technical expert deals with the issue of noninfringing substitutes and commercial success. Industry experts, including marketing employees of the parties, typically address the demand for the patented product, the manufacturing and marketing capability to meet that demand, and the commercial success of the patented invention. An accounting expert computes the amount of lost profits, considering incremental expenses and applicable gross margins, and any specific accounting practices unique to the patent owner or the industry. The accounting expert normally testifies as to the aggregate amount of lost profits and interest due.

In some instances, the patent owner pursues lost profits or reasonable royalty damages based on the "entire market value rule." In such a case, testimony of a technical expert is needed to establish whether the patented and unpatented components were analogous to a single functioning unit.

Patent litigation involves complex technical issues, unique practices and procedures before the U.S. Patent Office, and complex damages theories. Many of the issues in patent litigation involve mixed issues of fact and law. The complexity of the issues in a patent case strongly suggests that expert testimony is almost essential in assisting the trier of fact to understand the evidence and to resolve factual issues from the evidence.

Expert testimony in patent cases is under increasing scrutiny by the Federal Circuit, and the role of experts in patent litigation is still evolving. Nevertheless, the intent of the Federal Rules of Evidence is to permit expert testimony, even on ultimate issues, where it will assist the trier of fact in understanding the evidence or determining a fact-in-issue, subject to the considerations set forth in *Daubert v. Merrell Dow Pharmaceuticals, Inc.*[8] (i.e., the expert opinions must be competent, etc.).

In summary, expert testimony in patent cases always relates to consideration of whether the patent is valid and if the alleged infringer actually infringed the patent-in-suit. Expert testimony in patent cases can also be used in conjunction with preliminary injunction and summary judgment motions, as well as *Markman* hearings. Further, expert testimony can be used to explain the technology, to interpret prior art and claim language, to analyze issues such as infringement or obviousness, to explain the patent's file history, to explain patent practice, and to calculate damages based on reasonable royalty and/or "lost profits" theories. Therefore, the primary role of the expert in a patent case is to provide an understanding and comprehension of the complex issues that frequently arise.

Compensatory Damages

Once a patent is held valid, enforceable, and infringed, the issue of damages must be addressed. In patent cases, damages are provided by statute (35 U.S.C. § 284). A patent owner whose patent has been infringed is entitled to (a) an award of lost profits from sales the patent owner would have made "but for" the infringement; (b) a reasonable royalty on the infringing sales; or (c) a combination of lost profit and reasonable royalty. A reasonable royalty reward provides the floor below

8. 509 U.S. 579 (1993).

which damages cannot fall. Additionally, the patent owner is entitled to interest on the lost profits or on the reasonable royalty from the time of the infringement until the award is paid, and to the costs incurred in the district court litigation. Costs normally include amounts paid to the court, witness fees and travel expenses, fees for transcripts, and miscellaneous expenses. They do not include attorney's fees. Interest and costs are included to compensate for the infringement. Thus, the lost profits of the patent owner or a reasonable royalty on the infringer's sales, or a combination of lost profits and a reasonable royalty reward, along with interest and costs, are called "compensatory damages." Further, if the infringer knew or should have known it was infringing, then the patent owner may be awarded enhanced damages for its willful infringement, up to three times the compensating award, and may be entitled under 35 U.S.C. § 285 to attorney's fees as well. Damages over and above compensatory damages are called "punitive damages." The damages issue can be addressed by either a judge or jury.

A. Lost Profits

Lost profits are the profits the patent owner would have made "but for" the infringement. These additional profits the patent owner would have made, if the infringer had not been infringing, equal the patent owner's incremental profit margin in a "but for" world times the number of sales lost to the infringer due to the infringement. Proof of lost profits generally requires a showing that (a) but for the infringement, there is a reasonable probability that the patent owner would have made the sales; and (b) the computation of the amount supported by the evidence. The burden of proof on these issues is by a preponderance of the evidence. Any doubts about the correctness of the award are to be resolved against the infringer.

In determining lost profits, a test frequently applied by the courts requires the patent owner to prove:

(1) Demand for the patented product;

(2) The absence of acceptable noninfringing alternatives;

(3) The patent owner's capacity to exploit the demand; and

(4) The amount of profit the patent owner would have made.

When there is a two-supplier market, satisfaction of the first two factors can normally be inferred. Further, insignificant competitors and other infringers can be ignored. In a two-supplier market, demand for the patented product would normally equal the sum of the patent owner's sales plus the infringer's sales. Thus, in a two-supplier market case, the patent owner usually need only prove the third and fourth factors—its capacity to have made the infringing sales and the amount to which it is entitled.

Usually, "demand" for the patented product sold by the infringer is inferred from the fact that those sales were made. Other factors that have been considered relevant to the demand question include long-felt need and commercial success of the patented product.

The existence, or nonexistence, of an acceptable noninfringing substitute is determined at the time of the infringement. Thus, among other things, continued infringement after an infringement suit has been filed is evidence of the absence of an acceptable noninfringing alternative. To be an acceptable noninfringing alternative, the alternative must have all of the advantages of the patented product. Thus, the fact that a product is completed does not necessarily make it an acceptable noninfringing product. Even when there are acceptable noninfringing alternatives in the marketplace, the patent owner may still be able to establish its entitlement to lost profits based on its share of the market. However, the patent owner must still prove that its product and the infringer's product are similar and competing for the same customers. In such a case, the patent owner would be entitled to a reasonable royalty on the remaining infringing sales, those for which lost profits were not proven.

Regardless of the number of the suppliers in the market, the patent owner must establish that it had the ability to manufacture and sell the infringing products. However, in-place capacity is not required; neither is bidding on each product. The manufacturing capacity requirement has been met by showing that the work could have been subcontracted, that the patent owner's facilities were sufficient to manufacture the product, or that the patent owner could have expanded its facilities enough to meet the demand for the infringing product. The need to run extra shifts is not sufficient to prevent capability. The marketing capacity requirement has been met by showing that the patent owner had developed the market, protected its market and had substantial sales and advertising budget, employed direct salesmen, and is aware of sales techniques necessary to obtain orders from large corporate buyers. If lack of manufacturing or marketing capacity is due to the infringement, then the capacity requirement is considered satisfied.

The amount of damages need not be proven with precision, but cannot be speculative. The most straightforward calculation involves determining the dollar volume of infringing sales and multiplying it by the patent owner's gross or incremental profit margin. Fixed costs—costs that do not vary with increases in production—are excluded from the calculation. Examples of costs that are normally fixed are management salaries, property taxes, and insurance.

The amount of damages determined by multiplying the number of infringing sales by the patent owner's gross profit margin may not be adequate to compensate for the infringement. For example, the patent owner will generally be entitled to additional compensation if there is proof that, without the infringer in the market, (a) the patent owner could have charged more for its product; (b) the demand for the patented product would have been greater; or (c) the patent owner would have sold other nonpatented products along with its sales of the patented products sold by the infringer.

When an additional supplier enters the market, the potential for price competition increases. Price competition frequently results in "price erosion." If an infringer competed through price, it normally follows that the patent owner could have charged more, absent the infringer. A court can take into consideration what alternatives would have competed at the higher price. Evidence to be considered on this issue includes the relative prices charged by the patent owner and the infringer; a decrease in price or increase in discounting by the patent owner following the infringer's entry into the market; retarded sales growth attributable to the drain of substantial litigation; and the reasons why a bid was lost or won, as might be found in bid documents or the testimony of those selling the product.

Occasionally, the infringer will offer a product that is of a lesser quality than that offered by the patent owner. In such a case, that offering may affect the reputation of the product and, therefore, affect the sales of the patent owner's product.

The "entire market value rule" permits the patent owner to recover damages based on unpatented products that the patent owner would normally expect to sell with the patented product. Factors to be considered include the way products are marketed, price lists, industry practice of selling the unpatented product with the patented product, marketability of the unpatented product by itself, and physical dependence of the unpatented product on the patented product.

B. Reasonable Royalty

When lost profits cannot be established, the patent owner is still entitled to at least a reasonable royalty on the sales the infringer made of the patented product. By statute, a reasonable royalty is the "floor" below which damages cannot fall. A reasonable royalty award is normally determined by multiplying the infringer's total sales of infringing product by the reasonable royalty rate. The royalty rate to be used in a damages calculation can be determined by (a) constructing a hypothetical negotiation; (b) applying an established royalty rate; or (c) using the "analytical approach."

The hypothetical negotiation is based on the following premise: "[a] reasonable royalty is an amount 'which a person, desiring to manufacture and sell a patented article, as a business proposition, would be willing to pay as a royalty and yet be able to make and sell the patented article, in the market, at a reasonable profit.'" A reasonable royalty, in other words, is the amount the infringer would have been willing to pay prior to beginning its infringement in an arm's length negotiation.

The hypothetical negotiation cannot be treated as the equivalent of ordinary royalty negotiations among truly willing patent owners and licensees. Such an approach would ignore the cost of litigation and would impose a compulsory license on the patent owner.

In determining the reasonable royalty rate using a hypothetical negotiation approach, 15 factors are normally considered:

(1) Royalties received by the patent owner for the licensing of the patent-in-suit, proving or tending to prove an established royalty;

(2) Rates paid by the licensee for the use of other patents comparable to the patent-in-suit;

(3) Nature and scope of the license, as exclusive or nonexclusive, or as restricted or nonrestricted in terms of territory or with respect to whom the manufactured product may be sold;

(4) The licensor's established policy and marketing program to maintain his/her patent monopoly by not licensing others to use the invention or by granting licenses under special conditions designed to preserve that monopoly;

(5) The commercial relationship between the licensor and licensee, such as whether they are competitors in the same territory, in the same line of business, or whether they are inventor and promoter;

(6) Effect of selling the patented specialty in promoting sales of other products, the existing value of the invention to the licensor as a generator of sales of nonpatented items, and the extent of such nonpatented sales;

(7) Duration of the patent and the term of the license;

(8) Established profitability of the product made under the patent, its commercial success, and its current popularity;

(9) Utility and advantages of the patent property over the old modes or devices, if any, that had been used for working out similar results;

(10) Nature of the patented invention, the character of the commercial embodiment of it as owned and produced by the licensor, and the benefits to those who have used the invention;

(11) Extent to which the infringer has made use of the invention and any evidence probative of the value of that use;

(12) Portion of the profit or of the selling price that may be customary in the particular business or in comparable businesses to allow for the use of the invention or analogous invention;

(13) Portion of the realizable profit that should be credited to the invention as distinguished from nonpatented elements, the

manufacturing process, business risks, or significant features or improvements added by the infringer;

(14) Opinion testimony of qualified experts; and

(15) Amount that a licensor (such as the patent owner) and a licensee (such as the infringer) would have agreed upon (at the time the infringement began) if both had been reasonably and voluntarily trying to reach an agreement; that is, the amount which a prudent licensee—who desired, as a business proposition, to obtain a license to manufacture and sell a particular article embodying the patented invention—would have been willing to pay as a royalty and yet be able to make a reasonable profit, and which amount would have been acceptable by a prudent patent owner who was willing to grant a license.

Alternatively, in determining a reasonable royalty rate, the "analytical approach" may be used. This approach is based on a hypothetical negotiation between a willing licensor and a willing licensee, but focuses primarily on what the infringer would have been willing to pay. In certain cases, it can yield a very high royalty rate, particularly if the infringer's expectations prior to the infringement were high and can be proven. There is no requirement that the infringer actually make any profit, but rather only that it expected to do so. The analytical approach may begin with the anticipated gross profit of the infringer, subtracting the infringer's overhead expenses, allocating an acceptable or normal net profit to the infringer, and awarding the remaining profit to the patent owner.

Willful Infringement

Willful infringement is a finding of fact that must be proven by clear and convincing evidence. To willfully infringe, the infringer must have had knowledge of the patent and must then have proceeded to infringe without a good faith belief that the patent was not infringed, invalid, or unenforceable. Normally, the totality of the circumstances is to be considered when deciding whether an infringement is willful. The most important circumstances are those surrounding advice of counsel—including whether it was sought, when and from whom it was sought, and whether it was followed. Other circumstances that bear on the issue of willfulness are whether the infringer copied the patented product or rejected a license offer, and if the patent had previously been held valid. Bad faith is not necessary to find willful infringement.

Under 35 U.S.C. § 285, it is within the court's discretion to grant attorney's fees to a prevailing party in an exceptional case. Where the patent owner is the prevailing party, conduct of the infringer that may make the case exceptional is misconduct during the litigation or a frivolous defense to the suit. Further, an exceptional case has been established by proving, clearly and convincingly, a case of willfulness. Nevertheless, some element of bad faith or unfairness must be present to support the grant of attorney's fees.

Limitation on Damages

In certain circumstances, the amount of damages may be limited by statute or by the equitable doctrines of laches and/or estoppel. Under 35 U.S.C. § 287, damages generally cannot be collected unless the public was given constructive notice of the patent-in-suit by marking the patented product with the patent number, or unless the infringer had actual notice of the alleged infringement. The filing of the suit constitutes notice. The marking requirement does not extend to patented methods. If both a product and a method are patented and are asserted against an alleged infringer, then notice that the product is patented is required to collect damages for infringement of the method. By statute, the period for collecting damages cannot extend back more than six years from the filing of the suit.

When the patent owner has delayed in filing suit such that the delay is unreasonable, inexcusable, and prejudicial to the alleged infringer, then laches may prevent the collection of damages for the period preceding the filing of the suit. If the patent owner has delayed more than six years from the time it became aware of the infringement, then a presumption that the delay was unreasonable, inexcusable, and prejudicial arises. The burden of going forward with evidence to overcome the presumption shifts to the patent owner. However, the ultimate burden of persuasion on the defense of laches remains with the alleged infringer at all times. Involvement in other litigation or delay by the U.S. Patent Office are some of the justifications courts have recognized to rebut the presumption.

Equitable estoppel, however, may bar all damages, past and future. Equitable estoppel requires proof of (a) affirmative conduct by the patent owner (either action or misleading inaction), which led the alleged infringer to believe that it would not be sued for infringement; (b) detrimental reliance on the patent owner's conduct by the alleged infringer; and (c) material prejudice to the infringer due to that reliance, if the patent owner is allowed to proceed with its suit.

Section 282 Notice

Section 282 of the Patent Act provides that, in actions involving the validity or infringement of a patent, the party asserting invalidity or noninfringement shall give notice to the adverse party of the prior art to be relied upon at trial. The notice is required to be in the pleadings, or otherwise in writing, at least 30 days before trial. Notice must include the country, number, date, and name of the patentee of any patent; and the title, date, and page numbers of any publication to be relied upon in an anticipation defense against the patent-in-suit or in a showing of the state of the art. Also required are the name and address of any person who may be relied upon as the prior inventor, or as having prior knowledge of or as having previously used or offered for sale the invention of the patent-in-suit. In the absence of such notice, proof of the matters required under the notice may not be made at trial except as the court permits.

Final Pretrial Conference

A final pretrial conference is typically held before, but as close to the trial date, as is reasonable. The conference serves to formulate a plan for the trial. Pretrial orders are prepared in advance to extensively set out admitted facts, facts in dispute, a statement of legal issues (agreed and contested), a list of all witnesses, and all exhibits to be offered into evidence. A court order is entered that becomes a blueprint for the trial.

The importance of the final pretrial conference cannot be overstated. The court can be expected to address the question of how and when evidence will be admitted into the record, including a system for resolving evidentiary objections. In many cases, the court will already have required the parties to exchange exhibit lists and lists of objections prior to the final pretrial conference. The court may require that the parties attempt to resolve evidentiary objections and come to the pretrial conference prepared to argue or waive any unresolved objections. In a patent case, the parties can expect encouragement to agree to the authenticity of documents, unless there is a genuine issue as to an individual exhibit. Counsel should come to the final pretrial conference armed with a working knowledge of the judge's preferences with respect to handling evidentiary rulings and procedures.

A final pretrial order is entered after the final pretrial conference is held. The final pretrial order addresses several matters including the order of proof; the factual, legal, and procedural stipulations; the admissibility of exhibits; a detailed statement of the undisputed facts; and a statement of the factual and legal issues still in controversy. The final pretrial order can be modified only to "prevent manifest injustice."

The method of formulating the final pretrial order is within the court's discretion. Normally, a broad range of items are included in the final pretrial order, including:

(a) Statement of the nature of the action, the pleadings in which the issues are raised, and whether counterclaims, cross-claims, etc., are involved;

(b) Constitutional or statutory basis of federal jurisdiction, together with a brief statement of the facts supporting such jurisdiction;

(c) Statement of the facts that are admitted and require no proof;

(d) Statement of the issues of fact that any party contends remain to be litigated;

(e) Statement of the issues of law that any party contends remain to be litigated, and a citation of authorities relied upon by each party;

(f) List of premarked exhibits, including designations of interrogatories and answers thereto, and requests for admissions and responses, which each party intends to offer at the trial, with a specification of those that will be admitted into evidence without objection, those that will be objected to, and the support for any objection;

(g) Names and addresses of all witnesses a party intends to call to testify either in person, or by deposition, at the trial;

(h) Statement of what plaintiff intends to provide in support of the claims, including the details of damages or other relief sought;

(i) Statement of what the defendant intends to prove as a defense;

(j) Statements by counterclaimants;

(k) Any amendments to the pleadings desired by a party; and

(l) Certification that persons having authority have explored the resolution of the controversy by settlement in good faith.

Motions in Limine

At any pretrial conference, the court may consider and make advanced rulings on the admissibility of evidence brought to the court's attention through "motions in limine." Thus, the parties may make such motions prior to the final pretrial conference in order to exclude from trial evidence claimed to be inadmissible. One of the main purposes of motions in limine is the disposition of an evidentiary matter that might otherwise be prejudicial, outside the presence of a jury. Considering the issues raised by the motion outside a jury's presence enables the issues to be disposed of, without keeping the jury waiting or interrupting testimony at trial. Motions in limine serve other important functions, even when the case is not tried before a jury. Early decisions concerning the admissibility of evidence will often clarify a party's likely chances of prevailing on the merits and thereby may facilitate settlement. Further, if a motion in limine is granted, the nonmoving party may still have time before trial to develop an alternative line of evidence.

The effect of a pretrial ruling to exclude certain evidence is not always dispositive of the matter. Sometimes developments at trial allow for the admittance of the evidence despite the earlier ruling. It is important to reoffer, out of the presence of the jury, previously excluded evidence at trial. Failure to reoffer the evidence at trial may prevent the court's ruling from being reviewable on appeal.

Proposed Jury Instructions

The Federal Rules provide that at the close of all the evidence in a jury trial, or at such time during trial as the court directs, the parties may file written requests for jury instructions. Procedures for submitting requests for jury instructions are usually found in local rules or are left to the discretion of the judge. Typically, requests for jury instructions should be exchanged by the parties prior to the final pretrial conference and any agreed-upon jury instructions should be submitted to the court shortly before that conference. If the parties cannot resolve their differences as to particular instructions, each party is required to submit its own form of proposed jury instructions in the areas where there is disagreement, accompanied by citations to supporting authority. As a practical matter, proposed jury instructions should be prepared as early in the case as possible. The proposed jury instructions can be used as a guide to the legal issues and the evidence needed in the case, and early preparation helps to avoid the time drain of preparing the proposed jury instructions with the final pretrial order or at trial.

Types of Witnesses

Fact witnesses may be characterized in three categories: (a) friendly; (b) neutral; and (c) adverse. Friendly fact witnesses are those who have important and helpful information and would testify favorably and voluntarily at trial. They are normally employees or former employees of the client. Occasionally, witnesses employed by third parties may be friendly, for example, when their current employer has a common interest with the client, such as a licensee under the client's patent-in-suit, or a third party who, like the client, would like to see the patent-in-suit invalidated. Other friendly witnesses may have worked in the same technological area during the relevant time frame and now may be employed by another company in an unrelated field or may be retired.

Neutral witnesses typically work in the industry and are commonly employed by a third party in the same technological area as that involved in the litigation. Sometimes, although the preferred way of eliciting information from neutral witnesses is by an informal interview, determination as to whether such a witness may be important for trial testimony may not be possible except by taking a deposition pursuant to subpoena. This presents certain risks because the other side may elicit unfavorable testimony from such a witness on cross-examination.

Adverse witnesses are customarily employees or former employees of the adversary in the litigation or employees or former employees of a potential adversary of the client. Ordinarily, an adverse witness is not called to testify at trial unless his or her deposition was taken during discovery.

A good device for preparing friendly witnesses for trial is to set up a mock trial to help them articulate facts and events that best fit the legal theory and requirements of the case and effectively deal with cross-examination. The mock-trial testimony should be videotaped. An experienced trial attorney should act as the judge, an experienced trial counsel on the case should conduct the direct examination, and another experienced trial counsel should perform the cross-examination. The witness should be prepared on at least the major points for this pretrial exercise. Direct and cross-examinations should be limited to two to three hours and should cover all the key issues. The mock trial should be made as realistic as possible to simulate the actual trial court proceeding for the witness. After the mock testimony is completed, the witness and counsel can review the videotape and critique the witness's testimony.

The following rules can be used to prepare a witness for cross-examination:

(1) Pay attention to the question. It is important that the witness listen carefully to each question and think before he/she answers. Wait until the opposing attorney completes the question before answering.

(2) Witnesses should not answer any question that is not understood. Rather, the witness should simply indicate that he/she does not understand the question. If technical terms are used

that the witness believes may be misunderstood, opposing counsel should be asked to define those terms.

(3) If the witness did not hear the question or wants to have it repeated, say so. The question should then be read back to the witness by the court reporter, or restated by opposing counsel.

(4) Witnesses should not try to second guess where opposing counsel is going. If the witness does that, he/she may become confused. That could prevent the witness from understanding the question or the witness may answer a question not asked and may appear evasive.

(5) Witnesses should only answer the question asked. The answer should be direct and not evasive. The witness should not volunteer answers.

(6) Witnesses should not guess or speculate. If the witness does not know the answer to the question, the response should be "I do not know." This is proper and acceptable.

(7) If the witness is shown a document, they should take time to familiarize themself with it. The document should be read carefully before answering any question directed to its substance. The witness must be alert to an attempt by opposing counsel to lift statements out of context and use generalizations not supported by the document(s).

(8) Witnesses should not answer a compound or complex question. If counsel does not object to such questions, the witness should state that the question is too complex or involves several questions. The witness is entitled to have opposing counsel ask only one question at a time.

(9) If the witness cannot answer a question with a simple "yes" or "no," they should say so and explain why. Questions on cross-examination are typically leading or closed questions. That is, they seek a simple "yes" or "no" answer. If the question cannot be answered with a simple "yes" or "no," a fuller answer is appropriate. The witness, however, should avoid being hypertechnical or evasive.

(10) Do not view opposing counsel as attacking the witness personally. Emotional confrontations with opposing counsel are not necessary. It is important for the witness to stay calm and poised so that the answers are properly thought out and are not the result of an emotional reaction or outburst.

Trial

It is generally perceived that jury trials are more favorable to the patent owner since some jury verdicts for patent infringement damages have been very substantial. Compared to bench trials, jury trials require advanced preparation of jury instructions and more care in the development of exhibits, demonstrative evidence, and trial testimony. Jury trials typically result in a verdict and final judgment much sooner than bench trials. Moreover, a jury verdict is more difficult to overturn on appeal regarding its fact finding, assuming no prejudicial error in the jury instructions. Equitable issues that are typically not triable to a jury include an enhanced (up to treble) award of damages, an award of attorney's fees (35 U.S.C. § 285), and interest awards.

At the outset, there is no single "right way" to try a case. There are two goals in conducting a trial. One goal is to persuade the trier of fact, whether it be a judge or jury, to rule for your client's side. The second goal is to establish a record upon which findings can be made and supported on appeal. Prior to trial, it is very desirable to simplify the case into two or three issues of law and fact. It is also desirable to develop a simple theme or theory of the case. The theme will be the basis for developing a discovery plan, determining how discovery affects the theory and for outlining trial strategy.

For a case to be properly decided at trial, facts and evidence must be organized and properly presented. To be properly presented, facts and evidence must be properly prepared. Preparation begins with the first contact with the client and is part of the effort that should be undertaken to develop the theory or theme of the case. The theory of the case affects the choice of the forum, content and scope of discovery, determination of theories of recovery or defenses, issues to be argued and presented at pretrial, selection of the jury, content of the opening statement, direction and scope of direct and cross-examination at trial, and the closing argument at the end of trial.

Certain human phenomena are normally significant in the presentation of the case at trial. These phenomena are "primacy," "recency," and "attention span." Primacy is related to the concept that first-heard information is best retained. Recency is the concept that last-heard information is the last retained. Attention span refers to limits in the ability of judges and jurors to have sustained mental concentration. Most people only focus effectively for limited periods of time. Most individuals have attention capabilities of no more than 30 minutes.

The attention span problem can be addressed by use of physical exhibits and visual aids. This breaks up dull oral testimony and allows for points of focus. The pace of the examination and resulting testimony is obviously another important factor. Comprehension, however, can be adversely impacted if the pace is too fast and difficult to follow.

A. Witness Preparation

A determination must be made before trial regarding the order of witness and evidence presentation at trial. A decision must be made as to which witnesses should testify and in what sequence to provide the "story" you need to present to the judge or jury. There may be basic underlying testimony, providing definitions and background, that needs to be presented at the beginning of the trial to educate the judge and jury about the testimony to follow. Throughout the trial proceeding, however, the role of witnesses and evidence presentation is to educate the judge or jury on the client's view of the facts and issues of the case. The fact-finder must be able to understand the story from a factual standpoint. Expert witnesses, on the other hand, educate the fact-finder about specific technical issues of which they have expertise and knowledge. Fact witnesses are also educators, since they provide some of the factual basis and background upon which the experts later testify with their opinions.

After the witnesses have been selected and their order determined, a decision must be made about the exhibits that will be used during their testimony. An outline of the testimony of each witness is necessary. This must be done in consultation with the witness so that the testimony is correct and consistent with the witness's view of the facts. The pretrial preparation of witnesses also provides an assessment of the strengths and weaknesses of each witness and helps to formulate the questions that should be used at trial. These witness outlines form a roadmap for the direct examination and further preparation of witnesses prior to trial.

When witnesses are being prepared for trial testimony, potential problems should be considered. For example, based on pretrial deposition testimony and the opponent's trial exhibit list, a determination should be made as to what the cross-examination may involve. If, for example, parts of the witness's testimony to be presented at trial are inconsistent with that given by deposition, a determination should be made regarding the basis for the inconsistency and whether additional facts have been developed that may explain the difference in testimony. It may be helpful to present potentially damaging facts to your case through your witnesses so that you can put your own "spin" on them. This may be a better approach than creating an appearance at trial that the client was hiding facts, which may be the perception if those facts are brought out by opposing counsel. Thus, witnesses must be given as much guidance as possible about what they can expect on cross-examination at trial to avoid a situation in which the witness may leave the impression that he/she is not being honest.

An effective way to resolve or limit the problem with witnesses at trial is to videotape their testimony before trial and analyze it with them. Taking a witness through the entire direct examination and expected cross-examination allows the witness to review his/her own body movements, tone of voice, and impact upon the listener. By critiquing the videotape presentation and then repeating it with the witness, the witness learns how to strengthen his/her testimony at trial.

B. Jury Selection

Each jurisdiction or court has its own manner of selecting juries. There must be at least six jurors to deliberate. The court frequently has a set of questions that it asks prospective jurors. It is not uncommon for the court to request counsel to submit questions that they would like to have asked of prospective jurors. Most courts make available to counsel, before the time of jury selection, a list of potential jurors who will be included in the jury pool. This information can be reviewed in advance to provide information about the backgrounds of prospective jurors. After the court conducts its questioning of prospective jurors ("voir dire"), a short list of potential jurors is passed back and forth between counsel, with names being struck sequentially until a jury is chosen. Typically, the jury is comprised of six jurors plus two alternates. The process is not as much selecting a jury as it is deselecting or excusing jurors who are believed to be the most biased.

C. Opening Statement

After the jury is selected, the trial begins with opening statements by counsel for both parties. The purpose of the opening statement is to generally inform the court and jury of the nature of the case, what the facts of the case are from your standpoint, and provide a basis to enable the jury to understand, as the evidence is presented and the testimony is heard, the relevance they bear to the case.

The opening statement should be factual in content, not conclusory. This is the first chance a jury will have to form an opinion of the case that is being presented. An error in many opening statements is to proceed, in tedious detail, to list all the evidence the jury will hear instead of providing the jury with a simple story. The length of the opening statement depends on the case. Studies have shown that 80 percent of juries had the same verdict following opening statements as they returned following the close of trial. In fact, some of the best and most effective opening statements have been 15 to 20 minutes in length.

The opening statement should introduce the court and the jury to the parties and include a general and accurate statement of the facts in a brief and simple manner. Exaggeration of the facts and making unrealistic promises to the jury about the evidence that will be presented are errors that should be avoided. Jurors want to connect the evidence and testimony themselves, and therefore, the opening statement should provide an outline of the fundamental propositions of the case with an appeal to the common sense of the jurors.

D. Direct Examination

After the opening statements, the plaintiff's case in chief is presented through direct examination of each of its witnesses. Examination can proceed through a combination of narratives and questions and answers. The narrative is presented with a simple question followed by a lengthy answer in which the witness is the focus of attention for a prolonged period. The question-and-answer approach requires questions that call for short answers. Whether the examination is conducted using narratives, questions and answers, or a combination of the two, it is imperative that the testimony not appear to be rehearsed, since it is not likely to be considered credible by the jury. It is important that the testimony be as truthful and convincing as possible. The impression made by an honest witness is more lasting than any argument by counsel.

While the use of leading questions on direct examination to cover preliminary and noncontroversial issues regarding the background of the witness and setting the scene is rarely objectionable, questions that relate to the heart of the issue will be objected to if they are leading. By suggesting the answer in the question, the impact of having the witness present the facts is diminished. Jurors will wonder whether the witness would have been able to give the answer if the lawyer had not put the answer into the witness's mouth. Thus, it is best to mix narrative answers with question-and-answer examination to keep the focus on the main issues and prevent the examination from becoming boring. Short, simple questions that elicit direct responsive answers, asked at a reasonable pace, can be followed by any juror. Thus, the selection of an examination style, along with the use of visual aids and other demonstrative tools, is necessary to make the presentation interesting.

E. Cross-Examination

Cross-examination requires judgment, as well as the ability to know whether to ask the question and when to stop. An important tenet of cross-examination is that you should set specific goals. There are also specific rules to keep in mind. The first rule is that it is difficult to get a witness to change his/her testimony. Thus, it is risky to confront a witness about those matters that you believe he/she has truthfully testified to. Also, do not cross-examine the witness merely to make the point to the jury that there are questions that you can ask regardless of their meaning to the case. Some attempts to cross-examine witnesses provide a second chance for that witness to make his/her point. If the jury did not understand it the first time, they probably will understand it the second time they hear it from the witness. Therefore, do not ask questions that allow the direct examination to be repeated. Also, do not use open-ended questions that allow the witness to add to his/her testimony. Moreover, do not ask questions unless you know the probable answer before the question is asked.

Maintaining control of the witness is critical in cross-examination. This means that you must use leading questions at all times. The questions should be short, simple, and leave no opportunity for the witness to explain or ramble. Do not allow the witness a chance to elaborate. In selecting points to make in cross-examination, the summation or closing argument must be kept in mind. There are many examples of cross-examination in which the lawyer asked one question too many, and then heard an answer that negatively affected the case.

Cross-examination can be used to elicit additional favorable testimony that is consistent with the theory of your case. It can also be used to discredit the witness, discredit the basis or underlying rationale for the witness's testimony, cause the witness to be viewed as irrelevant, or permit the jury to disregard what the witness says. While the answers may not be what you wish them to be, do not argue with the witness. It is preferable to stop a cross-examination than to argue with a witness. Moreover, cross-examination is not a deposition, and therefore, it should not be used as a fishing expedition for something you hope might develop.

When cross-examining an expert witness, it may not be possible to discredit the witness with respect to the technology or background presented by the witness. Instead, it may be more fruitful to determine what the expert was not told or shown. If possible, the examination should demonstrate that there were facts left unconsidered by the expert, to raise doubt in the minds of the jury about the basis for the expert's opinion. Thus, attacking the foundation upon which the expert bases his or her opinion is normally more productive. Further, the scope of the expert's experience may be limited, such that it is shown that the expert is knowledgeable in another area, but is not an expert in the technology at issue.

F. Objections

Every trial involves numerous situations in which objections might properly be made. It must be recognized and understood that judges and jurors do not like frequent and constant use of objections. Jurors believe that lawyers who are constantly objecting are trying to keep them, as jurors, from hearing the truth. If, on the other hand, there is a solid legal basis on which to make an objection, you should make the objection in a simple, clear, and timely manner prior to the answer.

Unfortunately, important evidentiary objections need to be made to protect the record, i.e., preserve any error for appeal purposes, and keep the jury from hearing or seeing improper evidence. Errors that permit the admission of evidence at trial are usually waived on appeal unless a proper and timely objection was made during trial.

G. Offers of Proof

When an objection has been sustained that excludes evidence deemed to be important, you must make an offer of proof to preserve the record. The offer will also create a record so that the appellate court will know what the excluded evidence was and will be able to determine if the exclusion was proper or improper, or whether the ruling constituted reversible error.

One approach for making an offer of proof is simply to explain to the court, out of hearing range of the jury, what the proposed testimony would be. Usually this is in narrative form by trial counsel. Sometimes the witness will give the testimony through a series of questions and answers, out of the jury's presence. This provides a verbatim transcript of the excluded testimony.

H. Motions

At the close of the plaintiff's case, the defendant must move for judgment as a matter of law. This requests that the judge terminate the trial, in whole or in part, or enter judgment for the defense on one or more issues because the plaintiff has failed to introduce enough evidence to make a prima facie case. While this motion is frequently made orally, and will appear on the record, it may be a better practice to file a written motion. Similarly, at the conclusion of the defendant's case, after the defendant has rested, it is incumbent upon the plaintiff to move for judgment as a matter of law as to any of the defendant's defenses and/or counterclaims in which evidence has failed to establish a prima facie case. The defendant will renew its motion at that time or at the close of plaintiff's rebuttal, if any. A motion for judgment as a matter of law is submitted at the close of all evidence injury cases and may be renewed or joined with a motion for a new trial.

I. Closing Argument

The closing argument is the time to reflect on the evidence presented, reflect on the witnesses and their credibility, and to summarize the case. While many juries may have arrived at initial conclusions about who should win following opening statements, those conclusions can either be solidified or changed with closing arguments. It is perfectly permissible to comment on the evidence, on inferences that can be drawn from the evidence, and on the credibility of witnesses based on testimony elicited, both during direct and cross-examination. It is objectionable, however, to argue the law in a jury case, since the judge will instruct the jury through appropriate jury instructions about the law to be applied to the case.

Final arguments should review the theory of the case. The testimony of witnesses can be summarized and what they have said that is of significance pointed out to the jury. Closing arguments can be based on a logical review of the facts of the case where you have a strong fact case; and the facts, if accepted, will permit you to win. Another approach in closing arguments is to appeal to the sympathies and emotions of the jury. The most important factor with respect to closing arguments is that the person making the argument must be able to relate to the jury. If the presenter talks to the jurors in terms they understand, they will more readily follow the argument in their own mind and agree on the recollection of what developed at trial. Most cases are decided on relatively few controversial facts, but it is those facts that the closing argument must stress. Finally, it must be remembered that the attention span of the jury is limited, and therefore, the closing argument must clearly state what you want the jury to understand about the case.

J. Posttrial Proceedings

Rule 50 of the Federal Rules of Civil Procedure provides that a party may file a motion for judgment as a matter of law within ten days after the entry of judgment. The rule further states that a motion for new trial, under Rule 59, may be joined with a renewal of the motion for judgment as a matter of law, or a new trial may be requested in the alternative. A party must preserve its right to file a Rule 50 motion for a judgment as a matter of law by moving for a judgment as a matter of law at the close of all the evidence. Failure to move at the conclusion of the evidence waives the party's right to file a Rule 50(b) motion after judgment.

The U.S. Court of Appeals for the Federal Circuit was created in 1982. It hears all patent appeals from the federal district courts. The losing party in a patent case has the right to file an appeal from a final judgment in the district court. The record on appeal before the Federal Circuit consists of the original papers and exhibits filed in the district court, the transcript of the proceeding, and a certified copy of the docket entries. One of the more crucial undertakings in prosecuting an appeal is the proper selection of materials that should appear in the joint appendix. In the Federal Circuit, principal briefs are not to exceed 50 double-spaced pages and reply briefs are not to exceed 25 pages, exclusive of certain materials. An oral argument is normally held, heard, and determined by a panel of no fewer than three judges. However, if the issues involved in the case warrant, a larger number of judges may be convened. The Federal Circuit ordinarily allocates a party 15 minutes for oral arguments. Since counsel is normally confronted with an active and inquisitive panel, counsel must be prepared to answer a wide range of questions from the panel at any time.

All decisions of the Federal Circuit are subject to review by the Supreme Court pursuant to 28 U.S.C. § 1254 by a petition for writ of certiorari. The time for filing the petition is 90 days from the date of the final decision or judgment. The chances of the Supreme Court granting a petition for certiorari, particularly in patent cases, are remote.

SECTION V

Patent Proceedings

Proceedings at the U.S. Patent Office (USPTO)

An alternative to federal court litigation is found in the post-grant proceedings established by the America Invents Act (AIA). The AIA provides several "post-grant proceedings" that can only take place at the U.S. Patent Office. These proceedings offer the opportunity to reduce or eliminate unnecessary and expensive federal court litigation. The Patent Trial and Appeals Board (PTAB) acts as the decision maker for several post-grant proceedings. The post-grant proceedings can be initiated while federal court litigation is pending. This may permit the filing of an appropriate post-grant proceeding and simultaneous filing of a motion to stay the federal court litigation.

A. Preissuance Submissions

35 U.S.C. 122 provides for preissuance submissions to the USPTO by third parties. Preissuance submissions provide a mechanism by which third parties may submit patents, published patent applications, or other printed publications of potential relevance to the examination of a pending patent application.

The AIA expanded the rights of third parties to submit information in two important respects. First, the AIA expanded the time period within which preissuance submissions may be filed. Second, the AIA expanded the power of preissuance submissions to influence the prosecution of a pending application. Section 122(e) extends the time period for third-party preissuance submissions to (a) the earlier of the date that a notice of allowance is given or mailed, or (b) the later of six months after publication of the application or the date of the first rejection. For most cases, the AIA will extend the window for preissuance submissions from within two months of publication to any time before the date of first rejection.

All preissuance submissions must be accompanied by a concise explanation of the asserted relevance of each document submitted. The publication and explanation of relevance will be made of record in the prosecution history of the application, which may prove useful in a future infringement action. Further, there is no requirement that the real party in interest associated with the preissuance submission be identified. Thus, interested third parties can potentially affect the prosecution of a patent application, such as a competitor's application, without alerting the patent applicant to their identity.

B. Supplemental Examination

Section 257 of Title 35 provides for supplemental examination of an issued patent to "consider, reconsider, or correct information believed to be relevant" to an issued patent. Supplemental examination under the AIA differs from previous post-grant procedures in two primary respects. First, grant of a supplemental examination of an issued patent does not depend upon whether any deceptive intent or bad faith was involved in the failure to have the information considered, reconsidered, or corrected in the original prosecution of the issued patent. Second, the AIA calls for the use of supplemental examination to cure issues that may relate to an applicant's duty of candor and good faith before the USPTO, including the duty of disclosure prescribed by 37 C.F.R. 1.56. The ability to cure such issues during supplemental examination is subject to exceptions under the AIA.

Only the patent owner may request a supplemental examination of an issued patent. The request may be made based on any information believed to be relevant to the patent. Thus, the "information" is not limited to patents and printed publications, and may relate to other issues, including issues under 35 U.S.C. 112. The standard by which a supplemental examination is to be granted is if the submitted information raises a substantial new question of patentability.[1]

1. See 35 U.S.C. § 257(c)(1): "A patent shall not be held unenforceable on the basis of conduct relating to information that had not been considered, was inadequately

C. Post-Grant Review (PGR)

Post-Grant Review (PGR) proceedings permit a party, other than the patent owner, to file a petition to institute a Post-Grant Review (PGR) of the patentability of one or more patent claims for any reason (not limited to prior art issues). The petition must be filed by nine months after the date of the issuance of the patent plus the payment of a fee. The petitioner will not have standing if (a) the petitioner already filed a civil action challenging the patent's validity, or (b) the petitioner is estopped from challenging validity due to some prior action. That is, a petition for PGR must be filed before any civil action claiming invalidity and not more than one year after service of an infringement complaint.

Post-Grant Review is instituted upon a showing that it is more likely than not that at least one claim challenged is unpatentable. Post-Grant Review proceedings are conducted by the PTAB. A Post-Grant Review proceeding may be filed instead of or in addition to a federal court lawsuit. A petitioner in a PGR is free to raise any invalidity ground under 35 U.S.C. 282(b)(2) or (3). Legal estoppel may apply with respect to the outcome of the PGR.

D. Inter Partes Review (IPR)

Inter Partes Review (IPR) proceedings allow a third party to challenge the patentability of one or more patent claims based on grounds raised under 35 U.S.C. 102 (novelty) or 103 (obviousness). The challenge may only be on the basis of prior art consisting of patents, published patent applications, or printed publications. A petition may be filed after the later of either (a) nine months after the grant of the patent or issuance of a reissue patent, or (b) if a Post-Grant Review is instituted, the termination of the Post-Grant Review. The petitioner must show that there is a reasonable likelihood of prevailing with respect to at least one claim challenged in the petition.The IPR petition is limited in pages and must be accompanied by the evidence upon which the petitioner intends to rely for a finding of invalidity, and the payment of a fee. The petitioner

---

considered, or was incorrect in a prior examination of the patent if the information was considered, reconsidered, or corrected during a supplemental examination of the patent."

may not file an IPR petition if it previously filed a declaratory judgment action challenging the patent or if it waited more than one year after the patent owner brought an infringement action against it.

For both IPR and PGR proceedings, the patent owner is allowed an opportunity to file a preliminary response to the petition, which is due within three months of the filing date of the petition. The patent owner may choose to file a simple statement that it elects not to respond to the petition. The PTAB determines whether to institute a trial within three months of the date the patent owner's preliminary response is due or is filed.

The PTAB decides whether to proceed with a trial on an IPR petition using the standard: Is there a reasonable likelihood that the petitioner will prevail on at least one claim? The PTAB is required to conclude the proceeding, including trial, within one year of institution with the discretion to extend for another six months with cause. Discovery is allowed, but it is very limited in scope. The speed of the proceeding can cause the patent owner to take a position on claim construction to avoid invalidity, that precludes the patent owner's lawsuit claim of infringement against the petitioner's product.

A party may appeal a PTAB finding on claim construction to the Federal Circuit while a parallel federal court lawsuit is stayed. Legal estoppel occurs when the PTAB renders its determination on claim construction. The legal estoppel bars a petitioner from asserting, in any civil action, that a claim reviewed by the PTAB is invalid on any ground that the petitioner raised or could have raised in the PTAB proceeding. Estoppel also applies to the patentee under 37 C.F.R. 42.73(d)(3), since a patent applicant or owner whose claim is canceled is precluded from taking any action inconsistent with the adverse judgment.

E. Covered Business Method Patent Review (CBM)

A Covered Business Method Patent Review (CBM) is similar to a Post-Grant Review. The AIA specifies that a Covered Business Method Patent is a patent that claims a method of corresponding apparatus for performing data processing or other operations used in the practice, administration, or management of a financial product or service. The Review does not include patents for technological inventions. The AIA does not specify what a patent for a technological invention covers. Thus, the Patent Office has promulgated a rule for a technological invention. In determining whether a patent is for a technological invention, the following will be considered: whether the claimed subject matter, as a whole, recites a technological feature that is novel and unobvious over the prior art, and solves a technical problem using a technical solution. The petitioner has the burden to demonstrate that the challenged patent is a Covered Business Method Patent and that at least one claim of the challenged patent is not directed to a technological invention to show that the petitioner has standing to proceed.

Only a person or entity who is sued or charged with infringement of a Covered Business Method Patent may petition for a Covered Business Method Patent Review. A CBM may be requested except during the time period in which a petition for a Post-Grant Review could be filed. A petitioner for a CBM may request to cancel, as unpatentable, one or more claims of a Covered Business Method Patent on any ground. The AIA provides that CBMs will use the standards and procedures of a Post-Grant Review, subject to certain exceptions.

F. Derivation Proceedings

Derivation proceedings are like patent interference proceedings and are brought to ensure that the first person to file the application is the true inventor. Derivation proceedings in the Federal District Courts must be filed within one year of the issuance of the patent containing the allegedly derived claim(s). Derivation proceedings in the USPTO must be filed within one year of publication of the application containing allegedly derived claims. Estoppel does not apply.

Overview of America Invents Act (AIA) Proceedings at the Patent Trial and Appeal Board (PTAB)

The pretrial and trial schedule and format for proceedings under the America Invents Act is fixed by law. Since the schedule is expedited, the benefit of reducing costs may be offset by the patent owner scrambling after an unexpected petition is filed to find experts, take discovery, and prepare pleadings.

A. Filing of the Petition

The first step is the filing of the petition at the PTAB by the third party who is challenging the patent. Filing the petition is similar to filing a motion for summary judgment or a motion for preliminary injunction. It must contain all evidence, e.g., declarations and exhibits, needed to support the petition. The petitioner has an opportunity to file a response to the patent owner's submission, but the petitioner is limited to only rebutting the patent owner's evidence and argument.

To avoid successive challenges to the patent, the petition must identify the real party in interest. This requirement is also important so that courts know who is bound by estoppel. Identifying real parties in interest may cause jurisdictional challenges in the proceeding. For example, if the real party in interest has been defending federal court litigation on the same patent for more than a year before the petition was filed, the PTAB would reject the petition as untimely.

The petition should include an invalidity claim chart, and the petition should discuss patent claim construction. The PTAB uses a standard of "broadest reasonable interpretation of claims," which is a broader standard than the standard used in the federal courts.

B. Preliminary Response by the Patent Owner

There are restrictions on what a patent owner may include in its preliminary response, e.g., patent owners may not introduce testimonial evidence. The patent owner has the option whether to file a preliminary response, but, at a minimum, the patent owner must identify its counsel, and the real parties in interest must be identified.

C. Scheduling and Evidence

The PTAB has three months from the date the patent owner files its preliminary response (or three months from the date when the response would have been due) to issue its decision on whether it will proceed with the petition. In both PGR and CBM proceedings, the standard applied is "more likely than not" at least one patent claim is unpatentable. The standard applied in IPR proceedings is whether there is a "reasonable likelihood" that at least one claim is unpatentable.

The decision to institute identifies the claims and grounds on which the trial will proceed; it includes a preliminary claim construction ruling; and it includes a scheduling order. The petitioner has no right to appeal the denial of a petition, but the petitioner may file a declaratory judgment action in federal court.

The scheduling order provides a deadline for the patent owner to take discovery on the contents of the petition. It sets the schedule for the patent owner's response to the petition and for the filing of any motion to amend patent claims. The order also schedules the time for the petitioner's discovery of the patent owner's response and for filing the petitioner's opposition to any amendment of the patent claims. The order may also provide the schedule for filing a petitioner's reply to the patent owner's response.

All evidence must be filed in the form of an exhibit. The Federal Rules of Evidence govern the admissibility of exhibits in PTAB proceedings. Evidence is restricted to affidavits, transcripts of depositions, documents, and things. Motions to exclude evidence may be filed to exclude evidence believed to be inadmissible.

D. Discovery

AIA discovery is more limited than federal court discovery. Mandatory initial disclosures are required, and only routine discovery is permitted without prior authorization. Routine discovery includes depositions of the declarants and discovery of exhibits cited in pleadings or testimony that a party has submitted to the PTAB. Depositions are limited to seven hours for initial testimony (direct or cross); four hours for the following phase (cross or redirect); and two hours for the last phase (redirect or recross). Most depositions are taken regarding a declaration and are limited to the scope of the declaration. Routine discovery also includes the production of any information that is inconsistent with a position taken by the party in the proceeding.[2]

Additional discovery, that is, not "routine," may only be obtained by stipulation between the parties or by order of the PTAB when it "is

2. See 37 C.F.R. 42, Sl(b)(l)(iii).

necessary in the interests of justice" or under a "good cause" standard.[3] The PTAB rarely grants motions for additional discovery. It should also be noted that documents subject to a federal court protective order may not be used in PTAB proceedings unless the federal court judge allows it.

The PTAB adopted a Model Order Regarding E-Discovery that provides for limited production, which is substantially unlike the production of electronically stored information that is allowed in a federal court proceeding.

E. Motion Practice

The PTAB convenes a conference call within one month after the institution of the proceeding (PGR or IPR) to discuss the proposed scheduling order and anticipated motions. Most motions must be approved during the conference call as a condition to filing them. If a party discovers after discovery is underway that it needs to file one or more additional motions, it may convene a conference call with the PTAB administrative judges to obtain permission to do so. Motions include those to amend the patent, for additional discovery, and for joinder of additional parties.

There are requirements on the contents, page limits, and due dates of motions, oppositions, and reply briefs.[4]

F. Trial

The oral hearing before the PTAB (three administrative patent judges) takes place approximately seven to nine months from the date of the petition to permit the Board to issue its decision within the one-year deadline. The PTAB will consider the petition, the patent owner's response, and the petitioner's reply, and all associated exhibits, declarations, and transcript testimony in rendering its decision. Attorneys are not allowed to introduce new evidence at the oral hearing.

Live testimony does not normally occur at the hearing. The PTAB will require live testimony where it considers the demeanor of a witness

3. 37 C.F.R. 42.51(b)(2).
4. 37 C.F.R. 42.20–.25.

critical to assessing credibility. Cross-examination may be ordered to take place in the presence of an administrative patent judge, which may occur at a deposition or at oral argument. Unlike federal courts, the PTAB discourages elaborate demonstrative exhibits, and demonstrative exhibits must be served five business days before the hearing.

The AIA allows the introduction of statements and accompanying information (made or filed by the patent owner in a federal court proceeding) on the scope of the subject patent. A statement will be considered in determining the proper meaning of a patent claim. The statement may also be used to support proposed rejections of the patent claim(s).

The PTAB must issue a written decision within one year of the filing of the petition, with the opportunity for one six-month extension. There is no authority for the recovery of costs or fees. A disappointed party may file an appeal to the Court of Appeals for the Federal Circuit.

Request of Ex Parte Reexamination

Third-party requests for reexamination have been available since 1981 and continue to be available under the AIA. The patent owner or a third party, through ex parte reexamination, may submit one or more patents and/or printed publications that such person "believes to have a bearing on the patentability of any claim of a particular patent."[5] The request may be filed at any time during the enforceability of a patent, and the requester must establish that the submitted prior art establishes a substantial and new question of patentability, at which point the director will grant the reexamination request and order reexamination of the patent in question. The decision will be announced in the Official Gazette of the Patent Office.

The patent owner may, but is not required to, respond in a "statement," including any amendment to the patent and a new claim or claims the owner wishes to propose. The third-party requester may then file a reply to the statement. If the patent owner chooses not to respond

5. 35 U.S.C. 301.

with a statement, the third-party requester has no further opportunity to participate in the reexamination.

The AIA made changes to the ex parte reexamination. Statements of the patent owner, whether in court or at the Patent Office, taking a position on the scope of any claim may be submitted to determine the proper meaning of a patent claim. The director may stay, transfer, consolidate, or terminate an ex parte reexamination in the event of an IPR or PGR proceeding on the same patent.

International Trade Commission (ITC) Proceedings Under Section 337

Section 337 of the Tariff Act of 1930[6] is an important means for combating unfair practices with respect to import trade at the border. If imports are found to violate Section 337, the U.S. International Trade Commission (ITC) will issue an exclusion order to U.S. Customs and Border Protection (of the Department of Homeland Security) excluding those products from the United States. Section 337 proceedings, like proceedings under the AIA, are administrative proceedings outside of the federal court system and do not involve the assessment of monetary damages; the only relief available is an exclusion order. However, there is also the possibility of interim (injunctive) relief with a proper showing.

A patent owner may initiate a Section 337 proceeding by filing a complaint with the ITC requesting a Section 337 investigation. The ITC is a federal agency consisting of six commissioners appointed by the president and confirmed by the Senate. Once a complaint is filed, the ITC has 30 days to determine whether an investigation should be instituted on the basis of the complaint. The ITC is required by statute to complete Section 337 investigations at the earliest practicable time. To this end, at the outset of each Section 337 investigation, the administrative law judge sets a target date for completion of the investigation. The initial target date is usually set for anywhere from 12 to 18 months.

---

6. 19 U.S.C. 1337.

To prove a violation of Section 337, a complainant must establish (1) unfair competition or an unfair act, e.g., patent or trademark infringement; (2) importation, or sale after importation, into the United States of the accused products; and (3) the existence of a domestic industry relating to the product in question. In investigations that are not based on alleged infringement of federal statutory intellectual property rights, a complainant also must prove that the alleged unfair act has caused or threatens to cause injury.

SECTION VI

Claim Construction in *Markman* Proceedings

In 1995, the Federal Circuit found in *Markman v. Westview Instruments, Inc.*,[1] that:

> competitors should be able to rest assured, if infringement litigation occurs, that a judge, trained in the law, will similarly analyze the text of the patent and its associated public record and apply the established rules of construction, and in that way, arrive at the true and consistent scope of the patent owner's rights to be given legal effect.

The *Markman* decision requires that the court interpret the language in a patent claim and then instruct the jury on its meaning. It has become common practice for the court to make a *Markman* determination before ruling on any motions for summary judgment regarding infringement or validity. Many federal courts employ a separate proceeding to construe the claims as required by the *Markman* decision. During a *Markman* proceeding, the parties will identify claim terms in dispute and file briefs in support of their respective interpretations. The court generally holds a hearing after briefing is complete, during which a technical tutorial may be presented, if useful, and testimony of witnesses, including experts, may be offered. The court's ruling on the *Markman* hearing will determine the claim construction for the remainder of the case.

1. 52 F. 3d 967, 979 (1995).

SECTION VII

Glossary

Accused device
A device or product that is alleged to infringe a claim of a patent.

Alternative Dispute Resolution (ADR)
A method for resolving conflicts between parties other than litigation. Mediation, arbitration, and early neutral evaluation are examples of ADR.

Anticipation
When the disclosure of a single piece of prior art has every element of the claimed invention, there is "anticipation" (invalidity of a claim) under 35 U.S.C. § 102.

Apparatus claim
A claim of a patent for a product, structure, or machine. In contrast, a **process claim** is directed to a method or process, and a process that produces a product is referred to as a **product by process** patent claim.

Art
A standard usage in patent law for referring to a particular technology. **Skill in the art** refers to the ordinary level of proficiency in a particular technology. Under 35 U.S.C. § 103, a patent claim is "obvious" and unpatentable if the differences between the claim and the prior art are such that the subject matter of the claim would have been obvious at the time of the invention to a person having ordinary skill in the art to which the claimed invention relates.

Attorney-client privilege
Attorney-client communications are privileged from disclosure in discovery and at trial. This privilege extends to communications between corporate employees and in-house counsel.

Attorney work product

Documents prepared by an attorney or under the direction of an attorney before or during litigation.

Best mode

The inventor is required to describe the best method or best physical way known to the inventor for practicing the claimed invention.

Claim

A patent claim establishes the bounds of the technology within which the patent owner has the right to exclude others from making, using, or selling. For purposes of infringement, each claim of a patent defines a separate invention. A claim must be considered as a whole. The words of a patent claim define the invention, and only a patent claim may be infringed. The meaning of language used in a patent claim is solely a question of law to be determined by a judge, not a question of fact for a jury. The words of a patent claim are given their ordinary meaning; however, the inventor may be his own "lexicographer" if he sets out his uncommon definition within the patent disclosure. Infringement, whether literal or by equivalents, is determined by comparing an accused product with a properly interpreted patent claim, not by comparing an accused product with a preferred embodiment described in the patent specification or with a commercialized embodiment of the patentee.

Clear and convincing

The level of proof that produces in the mind of the judge or jury a firm conviction that the fact has been established. A clear and convincing standard is required in challenging the validity of a patent since a patent is presumed valid.

Commercial success

The commercial success of a product that is attributable to the patented invention. Commercial success may be relevant evidence of the nonobviousness of the invention.

Conception

A definite perception of the complete invention formulated in the inventor's mind. Conception only occurs when the inventor has all the required data and details for carrying out the invention.

Continuation

A patent application for the same invention claimed in an earlier application, by the same inventor, containing the same disclosure as the earlier application, and filed while the earlier application is pending. A continuation application is entitled to the filing date of the original application.

Continuation-in-part

A second application for the same invention claimed in an earlier application, by the same inventor, adding new matter not contained in the disclosure of the earlier application, and filed while the earlier application is still pending. A continuation-in-part application repeats a portion of the disclosure of the earlier application and adds matter not disclosed in the earlier application.

Contributory infringement

The act of knowingly selling a nonstaple article specifically made or adapted for use as part of a patented combination or for use in practicing a patented process. To be nonstaple, the article may not be suitable for substantial noninfringing uses.

Corroboration

The confirmation of a date of invention by additional evidence beyond the testimony of the inventor. An inventor's testimony, without more, is not sufficient evidence for the date of invention.

Definiteness of a patent claim

A claim in a patent must be "definite" and not vague. See 35 U.S.C. § 112.

Dependent claim

A claim that refers back to a previous claim and narrows the scope of the invention.

Enablement

The disclosure of a valid patent must, when the application is filed, give a sufficiently clear explanation of the invention so as to enable a person having ordinary skill in the art to make and use the invention without undue experimentation. See 35 U.S.C. § 112.

Entire market value rule
The recovery of damages for patent infringement based on the value of an entire apparatus containing several features, where the patented feature is the basis for customer demand for the entire apparatus.

Equivalents (Doctrine of)
An accused product or process, although not literally infringing, may still infringe if it performs substantially the same function in substantially the same way to obtain substantially the same result as the claimed product or process. The Doctrine of Equivalents cannot result in a patent claim construction that would cover the prior art.

Experimental use
An exception to the "on sale" and "public use" bars to a valid patent.

File wrapper estoppel
A limitation on the Doctrine of Equivalents that prevents the patent owner from arguing that an element of the accused product or process is "equivalent" to an element of the patent claim when, during the prosecution of the patent application (the "file wrapper"), the inventor narrowed the claim to avoid cited prior art. "Prosecution history estoppel" is the synonym for file wrapper estoppel.

Indefiniteness of a patent claim
A patent claim is "indefinite" or invalid if it fails to particularly point out and distinctly claim the invention. Definiteness is whether a person with skill in the art can understand the language of the claim when it is read in view of the patent specification. See 35 U.S.C. § 112.

Independent claim
A patent claim that defines the invention without referring to another claim.

Inducement of infringement
One who actively aids another in directly infringing a patent is liable for inducement of infringement.

Inequitable conduct

The applicant obtains a patent by misrepresenting or withholding material information from the Patent Office or submits false information to the Patent Office. Inequitable conduct requires proof of an intent to deceive. If inequitable conduct is proven, the patent is unenforceable.

Infringement

A person or corporation who, without permission, makes, uses, sells, offers to sell, or imports a product or process covered by a claim of a patent commits an act of infringement. See 35 U.S.C. § 271.

Laches

An equitable defense to infringement that arises when the patent owner inexcusably delays in filing a lawsuit against an infringer, thereby causing prejudice to the infringer.

Markman determination

In 1995, the Federal Circuit found that construing the meaning of language in a patent claim is solely a question of law to be determined by a judge, not a question of fact for a jury. In finding that the meaning of language in a patent claim is solely a question of law, the Federal Circuit found in *Markman v. Westview Instruments, Inc.*, 52 F.3d 967, 979 (1995), that "competitors should be able to rest assured, if infringement litigation occurs, that a judge, trained in the law, will similarly analyze the text of the patent and its associated public record and apply the established rules of construction, and in that way arrive at the true and consistent scope of the patent owner's rights to be given legal effect." The *Markman* decision requires that the court interpret the language in a patent claim and then instruct the jury on its meaning. It has become common practice for the court to make a *Markman* determination before ruling on any motions for summary judgment regarding infringement or validity.

Means-plus-function claim or limitation

A patent claim may recite "means for" performing a specified function instead of reciting an element in detail. The purpose is to provide a sufficient scope of protection for the invention without the need for a list of alternatives in the patent specification.

Obviousness

If the claimed invention can be readily deduced from the prior art by a person of ordinary skill in that technology, the claimed invention is "obvious" and nonpatentable. See 35 U.S.C. § 103.

On sale

If the inventor waits more than one year to file a patent application after a product embodying the invention has been placed "on sale," the inventor cannot obtain a valid patent. The one-year date prior to the filing date of the patent application is known as the "critical date." See 35 U.S.C. § 102(b).

Prior art

The body of existing technology against which an invention is judged to determine if it is patentable as being a novel and nonobvious invention.

Process claim

A claim of a patent that covers a method by defining a series of steps to be followed in performing a process.

Reexamination

A procedure where any person, including the patent owner, can seek a review by the Patent Office of the validity of patent claims on the basis of additional published prior art not previously considered by the Patent Office.

Reissue

The regranting of a patent in order to correct an existing patent that may be wholly or partly inoperative or invalid. A reissue may be requested because the original claims are too narrow and do not adequately protect the scope of the invention, or too broad. A reissue patent must be requested by the patent owner. An application for a reissue that enlarges the scope of the claims must be made within two years from the grant of the original patent. The duration of a reissue patent is coextensive with the unexpired portion of the superseded patent.

Secondary considerations

Objective evidence from the actual marketplace in which the invention is made. This evidence may consist of data showing how those in the marketplace viewed and reacted to the invention. Categories of secondary considerations typically consist of the following types of information: commercial success or the lack of commercial success of products covered by the patent claims; a long-felt need that was met by the invention of the patent claims; unexpected results achieved by the invention; the failure of others to make the invention; and the copying of the invention by others. There must be a connection between such evidence and the claimed invention. The independent development by others, or almost simultaneous invention by others, is a type of secondary consideration that is probative of the "obviousness" of the invention.

Terminal disclaimer

A voluntary giving up or surrendering of a certain period at the end of the term of a patent, which is primarily used to overcome an objection based on the rule against double patenting.

That which infringes if later, anticipates if earlier

A slogan that summarizes the two separate tests of patent law: (1) the test of infringement of a patent and (2) the test of what is anticipation in the prior art so as to invalidate a patent.

Venue

The place in which a lawsuit must be filed.

Willful infringement

The infringer knew of the patent and had no reasonable basis for believing that its actions were legal.

SECTION VIII

Overview of Proceedings Under the America Invents Act

Variety of Post Grant Reviews

	***Ex Parte* Reexam**	**Supplemental Examination**	**Post Grant Review**	***Inter Partes* Review**
Who can file?	Anyone	Patent owner	Third party only	Third party only
Basis	Patents and printed publications	Any grounds	Any grounds	Patents and printed publications
Threshold	Substantial new question of patentability	Substantial new question of patentability	(1) More likely than not or (2) novel or unsettled legal question	Reasonable likelihood
Timing	Any time after grant	Any time after grant	Within nine months from patent grant	Later of nine months after grant or date of termination of a Post-Grant Review
Estoppel	None	None	Yes—issues that were or could have been raised	Yes—issues that were or could have been raised

Trial Rules

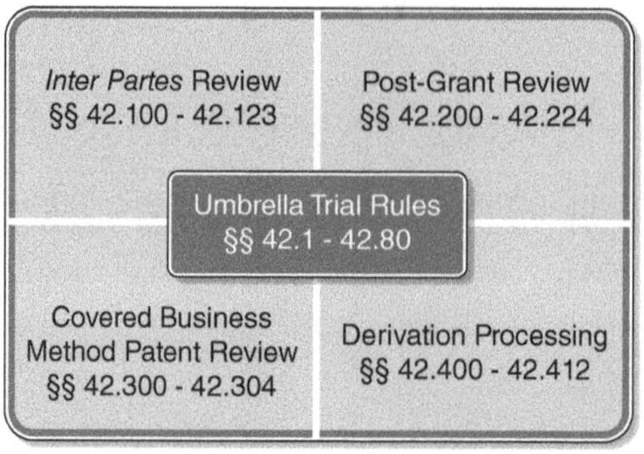

Trial Proceedings

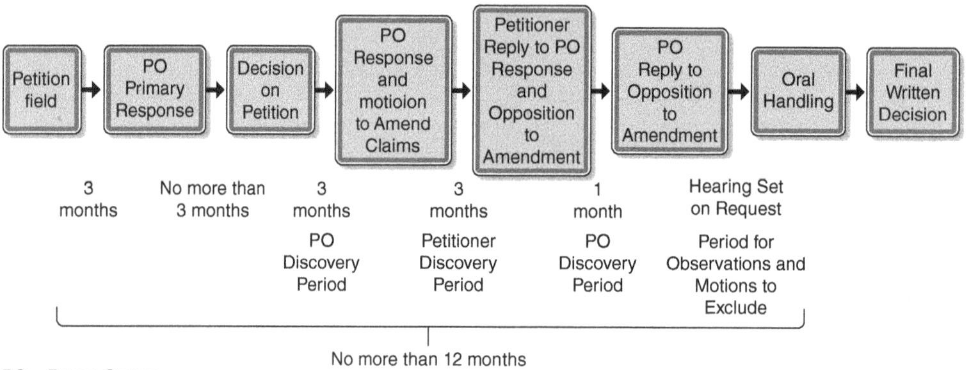

PO = Patent Owner

Major Differences Between IPR, PGR, and CBM

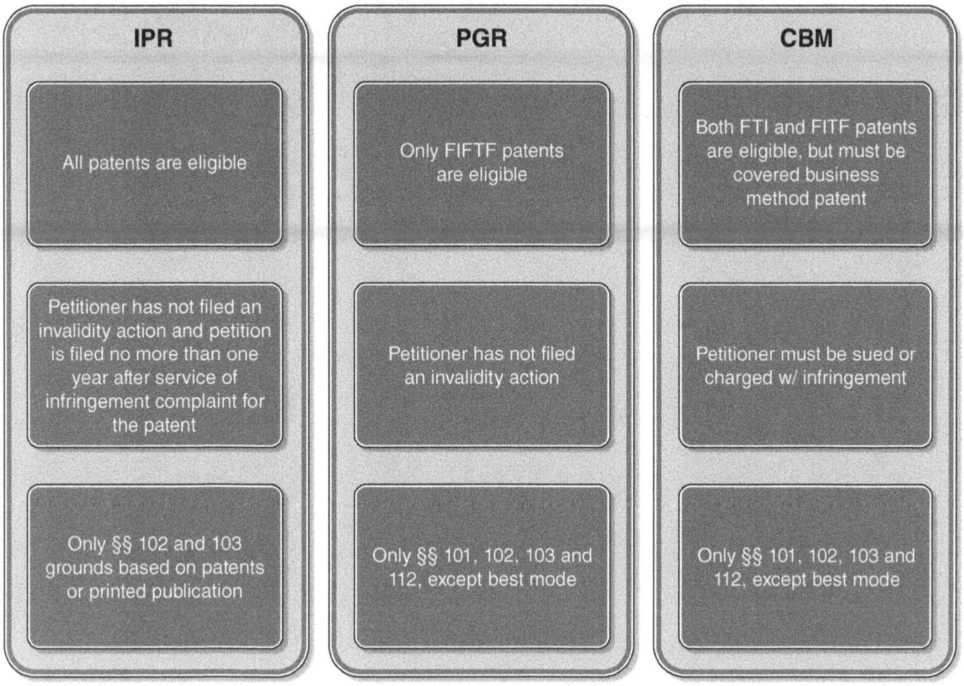

Threshold Standards for Institution

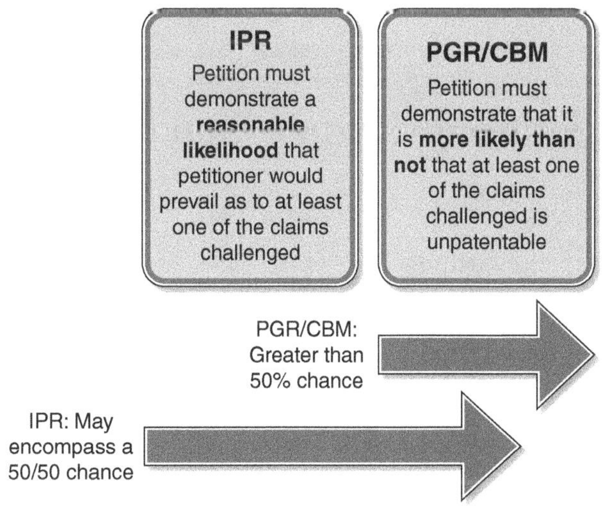

Time Windows to File IPR/PGR/CMB Petition

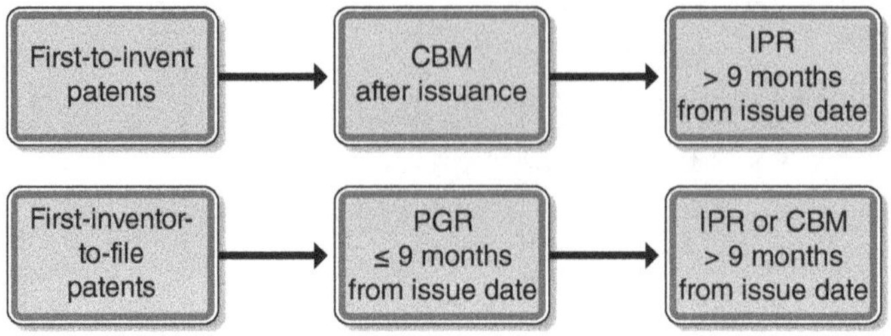

Inter Partes Review: Features

- All patents are eligible
- Third party who has not previously filed a civil action challenging the validity of a claim
- Request to cancel as unpatentable based only on patents or printed publications under § 102 or 103
- Filed after the later of:
  - Nine months after the grant of a patent or issuance of a reissue of a patent; or
  - Date of termination of any Post-Grant Review of the patent

Inter Partes Review: Petition Requirements

- Fee
- Real parties in interest
- Claims challenged and grounds
- Claim construction and show how claim is unpatentable
- Evidence
- Certify not estopped

Inter Partes Review: Patent Owner Preliminary Response

- Provide reasons why no IPR should be instituted
- Due *three months* from petition docketing date
- Documentary evidence permitted
- *Testimonial evidence permitted where interests of justice so require, e.g., to demonstrate estoppel*

Inter Partes Review: Threshold and Institution

- Reasonable likelihood that petitioner would prevail as to at least one of the claims challenged
- Board will institute the trial on:
  - Claim-by-claim
  - Ground-by-ground basis
- *Party may request rehearing*
- Completed within one year from institution, except the time may be extended up to six months for good cause

Inter Partes Review: Patent Owner Response

- Address any ground for unpatentability not already denied by the Board
- File, through affidavits or declarations, any additional factual evidence and expert opinions
- *Due three months from institution*

Post-Grant Review

- Most aspects of PGR and IPR are effectively the same
- Some differences as compared with IPR:
  - With limited exceptions, only those patents issuing from applications subject to first inventor to file provisions are eligible
  - Challenges may be based on §§ 101, 102, 103, and 112, except best mode
  - Only be requested on or prior to the date that is nine months after the grant of a patent or issuance of a reissue patent
  - Petition must demonstrate that it is more likely than not (i.e., a higher threshold than IPR) that at least one of the claims challenged in the petition is unpatentable

Covered Business Methods

- Employ the PGR standards and procedures subject to certain exceptions
- Some differences with PGR:
  - Cannot file CBM petition during time a PGR petition could be filed, i.e., nine months after issuance of a patent
  - Petitioner must be sued or charged with infringement
  - Petitioner has burden of establishing that patent is eligible for CBM review
  - Prior art is limited when challenging a first-to-invent patent

Covered Business Methods: Eligible Patents

- Both first-to-invent and first-inventor-to-file patents are eligible
- Must be a covered business method patent

- Generally defined in the AIA as a method or corresponding apparatus for performing data processing or other operations for financial product or service
- Definition excludes patents for technological inventions

Covered Business Methods: Technological Invention

- **Solely** for purposes of a CBM review, the following will be considered on a case-by-case basis:
  - Whether the claimed subject matter as a whole:
    1. recites a technological feature that is novel and unobvious over the prior art; and
    2. solves a technical problem using a technical solution
- *Based on what the patent claims, i.e., a patent having one or more claims directed to a Covered Business Method is eligible for review*

Covered Business Methods

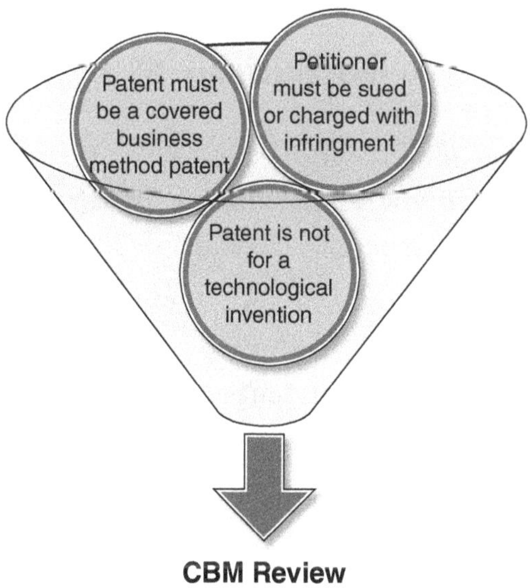

Derivation

- Only a patent applicant may file
- Must be filed within one year of the date of the first publication of a claim to an invention that is the same or substantially the same as the earlier application's claim to the invention. "The first publication" means either a patent or an application publication under 35 U.S.C. 122(b), including a publication of an international application designating the U.S. as provided by 35 U.S.C. 374

Derivation

- Must have a claim that is the same or substantially the same as a respondent's claim, and the same or substantially the same as the invention disclosed to the respondent
  - "Same or substantially the same" means patentably indistinct
- Must set forth basis for finding that an inventor named in an earlier application or patent derived the claimed invention

Derivation

- *Must certify that the inventor from whom the invention was derived did not authorize the filing of the earliest application claiming such invention*
- Must provide substantial evidence, including one affidavit, in support of the petition to show how the invention was communicated to the respondent
- Not likely to be instituted, even if the standard is met, until a patent with the claimed invention issues

Request

- Request for supplemental examination may be filed only by the patent owner
- Request may be filed at any time during the period of enforceability of the patent, e.g., generally six years after expiration of the patent
- Third party may not request supplemental examination or participate in a supplemental examination

Processing

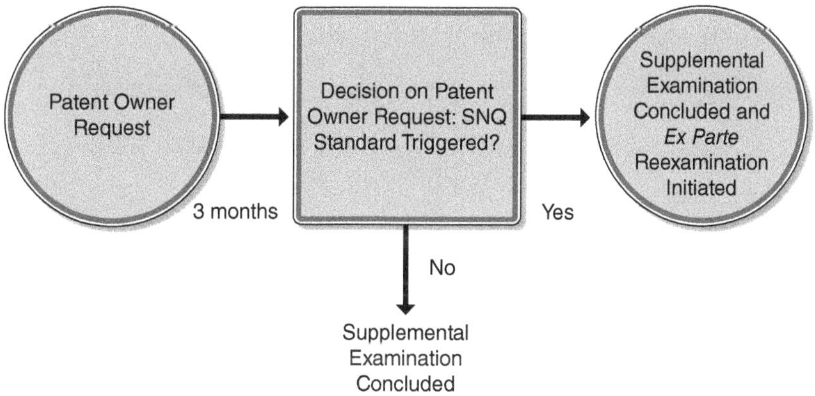

Contents of Request

- Identification of the patent and of each claim for which supplemental examination is requested
- List of the items of information requested to be considered, reconsidered, or corrected
- Separate, detailed explanation of the relevance and manner of applying each item of information to each identified patent claim
- Summary of the relevant portions of any submitted document, other than the request, that is over 50 pages in length
- Fees

Items of Information

- Information must be in writing and is not limited to patents and printed publications
- Request may not include more than 12 items of information
- More than one request for supplemental examination of the same patent may be filed at any time

Standard for Supplemental Examination

- If one or more items of information raises a substantial new question of patentability (SNQ):
  - Ex parte reexamination will be ordered
- If an SNQ is not raised by any of the items of information:
  - Ex parte reexamination will be/not be ordered; and
  - Ex parte reexamination fee will be refunded

Conclusion of Proceeding

- Supplemental examination proceeding will conclude with the electronic issuance of the supplemental examination certificate
- Certificate will indicate the result of the Office's determination whether any item of information raises a substantial new question of patentability

Ex Parte Reexamination Following Supplemental Examination

- Ex parte reexamination regulations govern, except that:
  - Patent owner will not have the right to file a patent owner statement

- Reexamination is not limited to patents and printed publications or to subject matter added or deleted during reexamination

35 U.S.C. 122(e)

- Any third party may submit printed publications of potential relevance to the examination of an application for consideration and inclusion in the record of the application
- Must be timely made in writing and include:
  - Concise description of asserted relevance of each document
  - Fee
  - Statement of compliance with statute

Filing of Submission

- May be filed in pending or abandoned nonprovisional utility, design, and plant applications
- May *not* be filed in issued patents, reissue applications, or reexamination proceedings
- May be submitted electronically via the Office's dedicated web-based interface or in paper but *not* by facsimile
- No service on applicant required
- Must be signed by submitter, but real party in interest need not be identified

Printed Publications

- Submissions are limited to "printed publications," for example:
  - U.S. patents and patent application publications
  - Foreign patents and published patent applications

  - Nonpatent documents, such as articles, Office actions, communications from foreign patent offices, etc. that qualify as publications
- Need not be prior art
- Best practice is to not submit documents that are cumulative of each other or information already of record

Statutory Time Periods

- Must be made before the later of:
  - Six months after the date on which the application is first published by the Office; or
  - Date of first rejection of any claim by the examiner

AND

- Must be made before the date a notice of allowance is given or mailed

Time Period: Example

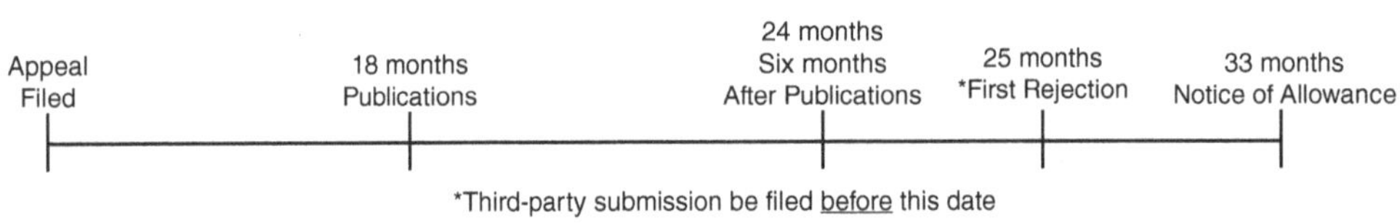

Contents of Submissions

- Document list
- Concise descriptions of relevance
- Copies of documents, but not for U.S. patents and U.S. patent application publications
- Translations for any non-English language documents

- Statements (1) of compliance with statute and rule; (2) that the submitting party does not have a duty of disclosure for the application; and (3) "first and only" submission (if fee exemption applies)
- Fee (if necessary)

Concise Description of Relevance

- Statement of facts explaining how the document is of potential relevance to the examination of the application
- Third party should not use the concise description to:
  - Propose rejections; or
  - Raise arguments related to an Office action or an applicant's response

Processing

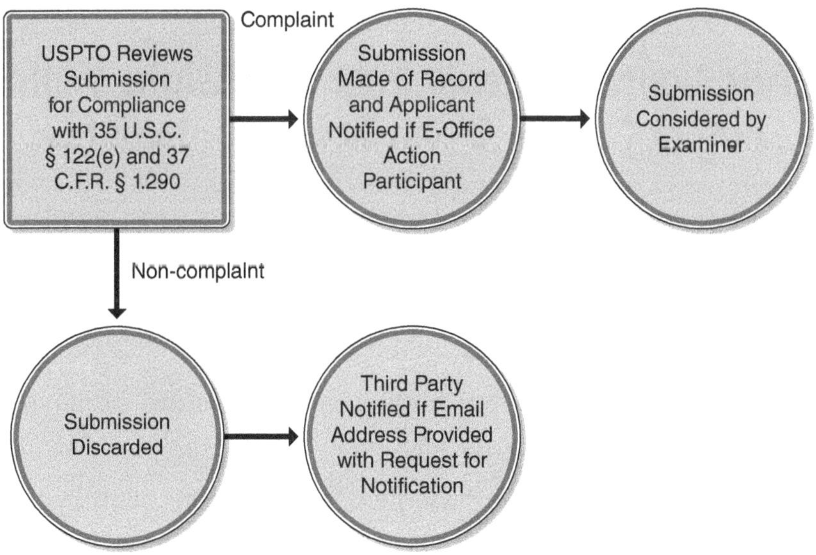

35 U.S.C. 301

- Expands the scope of information that may be submitted in a patent beyond prior art to include written statements about the scope of the patent claims filed by the patent owner in a federal court or USPTO proceeding
- Governs the use of such information by the USPTO
- Identity of submitter kept confidential on written request

Contents for All Submissions

- Prior art and/or patent owner claim scope statement
- Explanation of the pertinence and manner of applying prior art and/or patent owner statement to at least one claim of the patent
- Patent owner explanation may state how any claim is patentable over the prior art and/or patent owner statement
- Certificate of service on patent owner

Additional Contents for Submissions With Patent Owner Claim Scope Statements

- Documents, pleadings, or evidence from the proceeding that addresses the statement
- Identification of the forum and proceeding in which the patent owner filed the statement
- Identification of the submitted papers or portions of papers containing the statements
- Explanation of how the statement is a position taken by the patent owner in a proceeding regarding the scope of a claim

Office Usage

- USPTO will not use a patent owner claim scope statement in deciding whether to:
    - Order an ex parte or inter partes reexamination; or
    - Institute an administrative trial
- USPTO may take a patent owner claim scope statement into account after:
    - Ordering an ex parte or inter partes reexamination; or
    - Instituting an administrative trial
- To determine the proper meaning of the patent claims

35 U.S.C. §§ 315(e)(1) and 325(e)(1)

- Bar a third-party requester from filing an ex parte reexamination on the same patent after a final decision in a Post-Grant Review or inter partes review that was requested by the same third party (or their privies)

Ex Parte Reexamination Estoppel

- Request for ex parte reexamination must include a certification by the third party that the requester is not estopped from requesting an ex parte reexamination
- Real party in interest need not be identified in a request for ex parte reexamination

SECTION IX

Statutory Citations

35 U.S.C. 102(a)(1): Prior Art

- Precludes a patent if a claimed invention was, before the effective filing date of the claimed invention:
  - Patented
  - Described in a printed publication
  - In public use
  - On sale
  - Otherwise available to the public
- Generally corresponds to the categories of prior art in pre-AIA 35 U.S.C. 102(a) and 35 U.S.C. 102(b)

Grace Period Inventor and Noninventor Disclosure Exception

- Grace period exceptions under 35 U.S.C. 102(b)(1) for prior art under 35 U.S.C. 102(a)(1)
- 35 U.S.C. 102(b)(1)(A):
  - A disclosure made one year or less before the effective filing date of the claimed invention shall not be prior art under 35 U.S.C. 102(a)(1) if:
  - The disclosure was made by:

- The inventor or joint inventor; or
- Another who obtained the subject matter directly or indirectly from the inventor or joint inventor

Grace Period Intervening Disclosure Exception

- Grace period exceptions under 35 U.S.C. 102(b)(1) for prior art under 35 U.S.C. 102(a)(1)
- 35 U.S.C. 102(b)(1)(B):
    - A disclosure made one year or less before the effective filing date of the claimed invention shall not be prior art under 35 U.S.C. 102(a)(1) if:
    - The subject matter disclosed was, before such disclosure, publicly disclosed by:
        - The inventor or joint inventor; or
        - Another who obtained the subject matter directly or indirectly from the inventor or joint inventor

35 U.S.C. 102(a)(2): Prior Art

- Precludes a patent to a different inventive entity if a claimed invention was described in a:
    - U.S. patent
    - U.S. patent application publication
    - WIPO PCT application publication that was effectively filed before the effective filing date of the claimed invention
- Generally corresponds to the categories of prior art in pre-AIA 35 U.S.C. 102(e)

Noninventor Disclosure Exception

- Exceptions under 35 U.S.C. 102(b)(2) for prior art under 35 U.S.C. 102(a)(2)
- 35 U.S.C. 102(b)(2)(A):
    - A disclosure in an application or patent shall not be prior art under 35 U.S.C. 102(a)(2) if:
        - The disclosure was made by another who obtained the subject matter directly or indirectly from the inventor or joint inventor

Intervening Disclosures Exception

- Exceptions under 35 U.S.C. 102(b)(2) for prior art under 35 U.S.C. 102(a)(2)
- Exception 2 (35 U.S.C. 102(b)(2)(B)):
    - A disclosure in an application or patent shall not be prior art under 35 U.S.C. 102(a)(2) if:
        - The subject matter disclosed was, before such subject matter was effectively filed, publicly disclosed by:
            - The inventor or joint inventor; or
            - Another who obtained the subject matter directly or indirectly from the inventor or joint inventor

Commonly Owned Disclosure Exception

- Exceptions under 35 U.S.C. 102(b)(2) for prior art under 35 U.S.C. 102(a)(2)

- 35 U.S.C. 102(b)(2)(C):
  - A disclosure made in an application or patent shall not be prior art under 35 U.S.C. 102(a)(2) if:
    - The subject matter and the claimed invention were commonly owned or subject to an obligation of assignment to the same person not later than the effective filing date of the claimed invention

Joint Research Agreements

- Treatment of joint research agreements under Exception 3
- "Common ownership" exception under 35 U.S.C. 102(b)(2)(C) for 35 U.S.C. 102(a)(2) prior art is applicable if:
  - Claimed invention was made by/on behalf of at least one party to a joint research agreement in effect on/before the effective filing date of the claimed invention
  - Claimed invention was made as a result of activities within the scope of the joint research agreement
  - Application discloses the parties to the joint research agreement

Applicant Under 35 U.S.C. 118

- Permits an assignee, person to whom there is an obligation to assign, or person with a sufficient proprietary interest in the claimed invention to be the applicant
- Term "applicant" is no longer synonymous with the inventor
- Each inventor must still execute an oath or declaration

The Applicant

- Applicant may be the person:
  - To whom the inventor has assigned
  - To whom the inventor is under an obligation to assign (obligated assignee)
  - Who otherwise shows sufficient proprietary interest in the matter
- Applicant may also be:
  - Legal representative of a deceased or incapacitated inventor; or
  - Remaining joint inventor(s) if a joint inventor refuses to join in an application for patent or cannot be found or reached after diligent effort

35 U.S.C. 115

- 35 U.S.C. 115 requires for each inventor:
  - Oath/declaration executed by the inventor
  - Substitute statement with respect to the inventor, or
  - Assignment that contains the statements required for an oath/declaration by the inventor
- Phrase "inventor's oath or declaration" in the rules means an oath, declaration, an assignment-statement, or substitute statement

Inventor's Oath or Declaration: Statutory Requirements

- Inventor must state in oath/declaration that:
  - Application was made or was authorized to be made by the person executing the oath/declaration; and
  - Person executing the oath/declaration believes himself or herself to be the original inventor or an original joint inventor of a claimed invention in the application

Index

About the Author

Intellectual Property as a Strategic Business Tool

Terrance Rader utilizes his 30-plus years of courtroom expertise to consult with inventors, corporations, start-up companies, and law firms on intellectual property matters. With decades of experience, Mr. Rader is uniquely qualified to provide insights and recommendations.

Services

- Intellectual property analysis, strategies, and themes
- Outlining strategic intellectual property asset development, management, and commercialization
- Building cost-effective intellectual property portfolios
- Assessing the commercial and strategic business value of intellectual property portfolios
- Providing expertise in developing the appropriate intellectual property portfolio
- Identifying and evaluating new inventions
- Infringement and economic analysis
- Competitor intellectual property evaluations

Litigation Services

- Assessing strengths and weaknesses of the case
- Infringement and economic analysis
- Strategic consulting regarding options including federal courts and/or the U.S. Patent Office (AIA)
- Helping to develop an effective case theme
- Discovery consulting, including e-discovery
- Damages quantification, including lost profits and royalty rates
- Outlining questioning techniques specific to the case
- Witness consulting for fact and expert witnesses for discovery and trial testimony
- Arbitration and mediation
- Outlining approaches, goals, and procedures for mock trials
- Strategic pre-trial and trial presentations, including designing graphics and demonstratives
- Jury consulting, including jury instructions
- Outlining opening statements and/or closing arguments
- Appeal consulting

Multi-State Experience

Alabama
Alaska
Arizona
Arkansas
California
Colorado
Connecticut
Delaware
Florida
Georgia
Hawaii
Illinois
Indiana
Iowa
Kansas
Kentucky
Louisiana
Maine
Maryland
Massachusetts
Michigan
Minnesota
Mississippi
Missouri
Nebraska
New Hampshire
New Jersey
New Mexico
New York
North Carolina
Ohio
Oklahoma
Oregon
Pennsylvania
Rhode Island
South Carolina
Tennessee
Texas
Utah
Vermont
Virginia
Washington
West Virginia
Wisconsin

Representative Cases

Trial counsel in more than **400 federal lawsuits** involving intellectual property.

Tried more than **75 cases in 29 states,** including 21 jury trials, most of which were patent infringement actions.

Extensive litigation experience in **patent, trademark, copyright, trade secret, and unfair competition cases** in federal courts throughout the United States.

Supervisory Primary Patent Examiner—U.S. Patent and Trademark Office (1970–1977).

For plaintiffs: Obtained more than **25 multi-million-dollar verdicts or settlements, ranging from $2 million to $280 million.**

For defendants: Obtained more than 25 verdicts or settlements, which have **prevented potential damage awards ranging from $4 million to $400 million.**

About the ABA Section of Intellectual Property Law

From its strength within the American Bar Association, the ABA Section of Intellectual Property Law (ABA-IPL) advances the development and improvement of intellectual property laws and their fair and just administration. The Section furthers the goals of its members by sharing knowledge and balanced insight on the full spectrum of intellectual property law and practice, including patents, trademarks, copyright, design, and trade secrets. Providing a forum for rich perspectives and reasoned commentary, ABA-IPL serves as the ABA voice of intellectual property law within the profession, before policy makers, and with the public.

Books from the ABA Section of Intellectual Property Law (ABA-IPL)

AMERICAN BAR ASSOCIATION
Intellectual Property Law Section

Title	Regular Price	ABA-IPL Member Price
ADR Advocacy, Strategies, and Practices for Intellectual Property and Technology Cases, 3rd Ed. (5370273)	$179.95	**$144.95**
ANDA Litigation, 4th Ed. (5370274)	$395.00	**$355.00**
Antitrust Issues in Intellectual Property Law, 2nd Ed. (5370263)	$149.95	**$119.95**
Arbitrating Patent Disputes (5370229)	$89.95	**$74.95**
Biosimilars Litigation and Client Counseling (5370267)	$169.95	**$139.95**
Careers in IP Law (5370204) (The ebook is complimentary with ABA-IPL Section membership)	$24.95	**$16.95**
Commercialization of IP Rights in China (5370241)	$119.95	**$95.95**
A Comprehensive Patent Practice Form Book (5370260)	$139.95	**$109.95**
Computer Games and Immersive Entertainment, 2nd Ed. (5370239)	$89.95	**$69.95**
Copyright Litigation Strategies (5370228)	$369.00	**$285.00**
Copyright Remedies (5370208)	$89.95	**$74.95**
Crash Course on U.S. Patent Law (5370221)	$39.95	**$34.95**
The DMCA Handbook, 2nd Ed. (5370234)	$79.95	**$64.95**
The Essential Case Law Guide to PTAB Trials (5370233)	$249.95	**$199.95**
The Essentials of Japanese Patent Prosecution (5370245)	$149.95	**$119.95**
Intellectual Property and Technology Due Diligence (5370236)	$219.95	**$179.95**
The Intellectual Property Law Handbook, 2nd Ed. (5620154)	$139.95	**$109.95**
Introduction to Patent Litigation (5370277)	$99.95	**$79.95**
IP Protection in China, 2nd Ed. (5370270)	$149.95	**$119.95**
IP Strategies for Medical Device Technologies (5370238)	$149.95	**$119.95**
IP Valuation for the Future (5370237)	$89.95	**$59.95**
The Law of Trade Secret Litigation Under the Uniform Trade Secrets Act, 2nd Ed. (5370242)	$369.95	**$295.95**
A Lawyer's Guide to Section 337 Investigations before the U.S. International Trade Commission, 5th Ed. (5370266)	$139.95	**$109.95**
Legal Guide to Video Game Development, 2nd Ed. (5370227)	$74.95	**$59.95**
A Legal Strategist's Guide to Trademark Trial and Appeal Board Practice, 5th Ed. (5370275)	$179.95	**$144.95**
Marketing Your Invention, Product, or Journey, 4th Ed. (5370271)	$59.95	**$47.95**
New Practitioner's Guide to Intellectual Property (5370198)	$89.95	**$69.95**
Patent Claim Drafting Practice (5370259)	$179.95	**$144.95**
Patent Damages (5370276)	$79.95	**$64.95**

Title	Regular Price	ABA-IPL Member Price
Patent Freedom to Operate Searches, Opinions, Techniques, and Studies (5370230)	$139.95	**$109.95**
Patent Litigation Strategies Handbook, 5th Ed. (5370269)	$395.00	**$355.00**
Patent Trial Advocacy Casebook, 3rd Ed. (5370124)	$149.95	**$119.95**
Patently Persuasive, 2nd Ed. (5370272)	$139.95	**$119.95**
The Practitioner's Guide to the PCT, 2nd Ed. (5370261)	$139.95	**$109.95**
The Practitioner's Guide to Trials Before the Patent Trial and Appeal Board, 3rd Ed. (5370258)	$169.95	**$139.95**
Pre-ANDA Litigation, 3rd Ed. (5370256)	$349.00	**$259.00**
Preliminary Relief in Patent Infringement Disputes (5370194)	$119.95	**$94.95**
Principles of Patent Claim Drafting and Patent Claim Analysis (5370268)	$159.95	**$127.95**
Right of Publicity (5370215)	$89.95	**$74.95**
Settlement of Patent Litigation and Disputes (5370192)	$179.95	**$144.95**
Starting an IP Law Practice (5370202)	$54.95	**$34.95**
Summary of Covenants Not to Compete (5370244)	$179.95	**$144.95**
The Tech Contracts Handbook, 3rd Ed. (5370248)	$42.95	**$33.95**
Trademark and Deceptive Advertising Surveys, 2nd Ed. (5370255)	$189.95	**$151.95**
What Is a Copyright, 4th Ed. (5370257)	$19.95	**$16.95**
What Is a Patent, 4th Ed. (5370262)	$19.95	**$16.95**
What Is a Trademark, 5th Ed. (5370254)	$19.95	**$16.95**
What Is a Trade Secret (5370265)	$19.95	**$16.95**

Find these and other ABA-IPL books at ShopABA.com

Thank you for your order!

Jeff Salyards
Executive Editor, ABA Publishing
jeff.salyards@americanbar.org

Tax, shipping and handling charges may apply.
See web store for complete details and current shipping and handling rates and information.

2 EASY WAYS TO ORDER **ShopABA.org** OR **(800) 285-2221**